sous vide
for the home cook

Douglas E. Baldwin

Paradox Press

To my parents

I cannot thank my parents, LaVaun and Richard, enough for helping me at every stage in writing this book. Mary Dan Eades for her excellent and exhaustive editing of this book. Mark Ablowitz for giving me the time off from my research to finish this book.

I would also like to thank the following people for all their helpful suggestions: Alexander Wood, Alf Lervåg, Beth Price, Connie Brandau, Dean Grumlose, Derek Slager, Don Truitt, Douglas Wallace, Dudley Harde, Edmund Wong, Elias Pontikos, Erik Jacobs, Frank Kurzawa, Hank Sawtelle, Jason Baker, Joern Kalter, Larry Lofthouse, Leslie Smith, Marilyn Boyd, Martin Lersch, Moura Quinn, Nick Reynolds, Peter Gruber, Pete Snyder, Sharon Kissack, Stacy LeRoche, Su Sayre, and William Schreiner.

Contents

Contents

Contents

Contents

Foreword

The technique of sous vide cooking was first developed in France in the 1970s by Chef Georges Pralus, initially as a means for optimally cooking—and minimizing costly shrinkage—of foie gras in the commercial kitchen, where saving an ounce here and a few grams there goes straight to the bottom line. Medallions of foie gras, vacuum-sealed in food-grade plastic, and immersed in a gently and precisely heated water bath shrink far less, reducing food costs, and increasing profitability. Initially it was about business smarts, but the true power of the technique lay beyond dollars, francs, and pounds. Foods cooked this way were simply transcendent in flavor and integrity.

The method quickly expanded from that narrow beginning and has become the mainstay of elite chefs world wide, including such notables as Heston Blumenthal in the UK and Thomas Keller in the US, as a means of leveraging their time and skills to reproducibly cook a wide range of foods to near perfection night after night. Unlike the home kitchen, in a restaurant, a dozen diners may walk through the door almost simultaneously, each wanting a different entrée, cooked perfectly. One head chef with a small staff could manage it only by employing a precook-chill-finish method. And for that purpose, sous vide reigns supreme. And so, it took its place of importance in the elite chef's kitchen.

Being in the health and nutrition business for many years, we were acquainted with the concept of sous vide cooking, but had not thought to attempt it ourselves until a few years ago, when we enjoyed a remarkable double cut pork chop from the room service menu of a Las Vegas hotel. In our experience 'room service' and 'remarkable' don't usually appear in the same sentence, but this pork chop was tender, meaty, moist, and perfectly cooked from edge to edge with a crispy, golden sear on just the surface. It was, perhaps, the best pork chop we'd ever eaten. So much so, that the next morning, we dropped by the restaurant to inquire how it was cooked and were told it was prepared sous vide.

So memorable, in fact, was that chop, that when we returned home, we decided to try the method ourselves and went online to read more about it. We rigged up a contraption made of a large stockpot balanced atop a simmering ring from an old stove-top wok, over the lowest flame our gas burner would allow. We filled the pot with water, clipped a candy thermometer to the rim, and heated the water to 140°F/60°C. Using our kitchen vacuum sealer, we seasoned and sealed a pair of chops and popped them into the pot. Now came the real work: an hour of vigilance, of standing, stirring, adding ice cubes, adding hot water and attempting to keep the water bath at a constant temperature.

The result was a slightly overdone, but moist and tender chop, since it's almost impossible to maintain a constant temperature that way. Our experiment taught us two things: we now know that 140°F is too warm for our taste in chops; we prefer them cooked slightly cooler, more like 134°F or 135°F and that it's a real pain to constantly tend the bath for an hour or more. That sent us scurrying off to purchase a machine to do the work for us. Finding only very expensive machines designed for the commercial kitchen sent us in yet another direction—into the small appliance development business. And from that venture came the world's first (and in our opinion, finest) water oven designed specifically for the home kitchen: The SousVide Supreme.™

So now, the home cook had an affordable machine for cooking sous vide, but what was missing was a cookbook designed for cooking sous vide at home. There are but a few cookbooks about the sous vide technique on the market at present—Thomas Keller's *Under Pressure* and Joan Roca's *Sous-Vide Cuisine* being the most renown—but while beautiful to look at and entertaining to read, they are written for chefs. Neither really speaks to how average people cook at home or tells the everyday cook how to use this technique.

All that changes with this book by Douglas Baldwin—a PhD candidate in mathematics, part scientist, part good cook—who labels himself the Mathematical Chef. In *Sous Vide for the Home Cook*, Mr. Baldwin has given a blue print for simple sous vide cooking to all of us non-chefs wanting to attempt the sous vide technique ourselves. Everyone from the accomplished cook to the rank novice can reliably turn out delicious sous vide meals time after time using his easy to follow recipes for everything from meats, poultry, fish and game to the gamut of veggies and even desserts. His time and temperature tables for cooking, pasteurizing, and chilling are a tour de force that could only have been accomplished by an individual devoted, by nature, to such extreme mathematical precision. The mathematician in him is evident, too, in the painstaking research he undertook to match specific flavor combinations of the spices and herbs used in his sauces with the proteins best suited to them.

For those of us using this wonderful book there will be an added bonus: free time. Because so much of sous vide cooking is hands off and because the method is gentle and forgiving, it will leverage the limited time of the busy home cook, making it easy to have perfectly cooked, restaurant quality meals ready in minutes after the workday and more time to devote to other pursuits. Moreover, harkening back to its origins, it will even save money, easing the strain on tight budgets, by making tough cuts, such as flank steak or brisket, as tender as filet mignon for a fraction of the cost.

The home kitchen will never be the same.

~Drs. Michael and Mary Dan Eades
February 2010

The Basics

Sous vide cooking is about mastering temperature.

Almost any food you cook or bake, regardless of the method, will be its best within only a very narrow temperature range:

- meat is only medium-rare if the highest temperature it reaches is 130–135°F (55–57°C);
- fish is only moist and flaky if it never exceeds 140–145°F (60–63°C); and
- custards set around 175°F (80°C) and curdle over about 185°F (85°C).

In conventional cooking, your heat source (oven, cooktop, grill, etc.) is always much hotter than your food's ideal temperature. This huge difference in temperature means, for instance, that the time between an under- and an over-cooked steak is often less than a minute. But if you decrease this difference in temperature, the time between your food's being under- and over-cooked increases. So much so, that food cooked at its ideal temperature can never overcook!

This is the first tenet of sous vide cooking: *for the best results, always cook your food at its ideal temperature.*

With any new technique, the best way to learn is by doing. In this chapter you'll learn: Doneness only depends on temperature. Making food safe depends on both temperature and time. Searing food cooked sous vide at a very high temperature will keep it moist and give it great flavor. Cooking an inexpensive chuck roast for 24 hours will make it as tender as prime rib. Sous vide can make incredible barbecued pulled pork. And sous vide carrots and potatoes are easy and delicious.

The Basics of Cooking Eggs

Cooking food at its ideal temperature requires special equipment. Setting a conventional heat source (oven, cooktop, grill, etc.) to the food's ideal temperature is not an option, because they're neither precise enough nor efficient enough. Most sous vide cooking is done in a special water bath that can keep the water to within 1°F (0.5°C) of the set temperature. Water is used because it conducts heat twenty-four times faster than air and four times faster than oil, which means the food comes up to temperature fairly quickly; this difference in thermal conductivity is why water at room temperature feels cooler than air at the same temperature.

Learn by Doing: Soft-Boiled Eggs

The perfect soft-boiled egg has stymied chefs for centuries. If, as the name suggests, you put the egg into boiling water, then the difference in cooking time between a perfect custardy yolk and a hard yolk is about 30 seconds. Moreover, the largest egg in a typical dozen takes around 1½ minutes longer than the smallest egg. Combine these two facts and you may conclude that consistently getting a perfect soft-boiled egg is impossible!

But if, instead of boiling the egg, you use your precision water bath to cook the egg at its ideal temperature, then it's a whole new game. Since the yolk in a chicken egg changes from a liquid to a custard-like gel at 148°F (64.5°C), fill your water bath with fresh water and set the temperature to 148°F (64.5°C). Once your water bath has come up to temperature, gently lower a chicken egg (in its shell) into the water and cook it for 45 minutes to an hour. Remove the egg from the water and crack it open with a table knife or a teaspoon. You'll find the white has just barely set and the yolk is the consistency of custard. If the yolk is runny, then you'll need to recalibrate your water bath. (Instructions for calibrating your water bath are given on page 249.) And unlike traditional boiling water methods for cooking eggs, time is not a critical factor. Even if you were to cook the egg in the water bath overnight, the yolk would still have this same custard-like texture.

This "perfect" egg shows us that, for some foods, doneness only depends on the highest temperature the food reaches.

Science: Cooking Eggs in Their Shells

When an egg is cooked in its shell, heat causes different proteins in the egg to denature. Denaturing just means the shape of the protein has been altered by heat or chemicals (such as acids and salts). In a raw egg, the proteins are in tight bundles. As the egg is heated, some of these bundles are able to unfold or extend. This unfolding causes the liquid in the egg white and yolk to gel. One way to visualize this gelling is to imagine a container filled with hundreds of ping-pong balls (water molecules) and a dozen balls of yarn (proteins); now imagine the balls of yarn unwinding, getting tangled together, and trapping the ping-pong balls within the network of tangled yarn.

The important temperatures and proteins when cooking an egg in its shell are:

- *143°F (61.5°C): the protein conalbumin denatures and causes the egg white to form a loose gel;*
- *148°F (64.5°C): the protein livetin denatures and causes the egg yolk to form a tender gel;*
- *158°F (70°C): the protein ovomucoid denatures and causes the egg white to form a firm gel (the egg yolk also coagulates around this temperature); and*
- *184°F (84.5°C): the protein ovalbumin denatures and causes the egg white to become rubbery.*

If you like your egg white firmer than it is in the "perfect" egg, heat the water bath to 167°F (75°C) and cook the egg for the time listed in Table 1 on page 162.

The Basics of Cooking Fish

Food cooked sous vide is vacuum-sealed in food-grade, heat-stable, plastic pouches to keep the nutrients and flavors from leaching out of the food and into the water; hence foods cooked sous vide are especially flavorful and nutritious. It's this vacuum-sealing of the food that gives sous vide, which is French for "under vacuum," its name.

Removing most of the air from the pouch has several other important benefits: most importantly it holds the plastic tightly against the food so the energy from the water can be efficiently transferred to the food. If air is left in the pouch, then it will cause the pouch to float and keep the food from being cooked evenly throughout. Vacuum-sealing the food also reduces off-flavors from oxidation and prevents the food from being re-contaminated after cooking. For a detailed discussion of the equipment and techniques necessary for vacuum-sealing food for sous vide cooking, see page 250.

Learn by Doing: Fish Fillets

Fish starts to flake around 113°F (45°C) and remains moist and tender up to about 145°F (63°C). But unless you're buying sushi-grade fish that's impeccably fresh, you'll need to cook the fish at 130°F (55°C) or higher until you have reduced any harmful food pathogens or parasites to a safe level.

Cooking food to reduce harmful pathogens (mostly bacteria) to a safe level is called pasteurization. The time needed to pasteurize a piece of food decreases rapidly as the temperature increases: milk can be pasteurized at 145°F (62°C) for 30 minutes or at 161°F (72°C) for 15 seconds. Since the common food pathogens, Clostridium perfringens, can grow at temperatures up to 126.1°F (52.3°C), the lowest practical temperature that food can be pasteurized at is 130°F (55°C). Unless otherwise noted, all the recipes in this cookbook specify a cooking time that will pasteurize the food. When pasteurizing, you should start timing after the water bath has returned to its set temperature.

This is the second tenet of sous vide cooking: *unless you would be willing to eat the food raw, you must cook it at 130°F (55°C) or higher until any harmful pathogens in the food have been reduced to a safe level.*

In selecting fish, select a piece of fish that still smells of the sea and has flesh that's shiny, moist, and firm to the touch. Ask your fish-monger for a bag of ice and keep the fish on the ice (even in your refrigerator) until you're ready to cook it. You may also want to ask your fish-monger to remove the skin and any remaining pin-bones from the fillet.

Although many people prefer fish cooked at lower temperatures, cooking fish at 140°F (60°C) provides a good balance between taste and safety. So, for this learning exercise, preheat your water bath to 140°F (60°C). Vacuum-seal your fish fillet in a plastic pouch. Put the sealed pouch into the preheated water bath and cook the fillet for 40–50 minutes. A few minutes before serving the fish, melt some butter in a microwave and stir in a little finely minced or pressed garlic. Remove the fillet from its pouch and top it with the garlic butter and a pinch of salt and pepper.

You will find that the fish is moist, flaky, and has great flavor. Moreover, because it was vacuum-sealed in a pouch and pasteurized at a lower temperature, it retained significantly more vitamins, minerals, and healthful omega-3 fatty acids than traditionally cooked fish.

The Basics of Cooking Meat & Poultry

The flavor of cooked meat, poultry, and fish comes from the breakdown of fats by heat and oxygen and from the browning of proteins in lean tissues (a process called the Maillard reaction, see *Science: The Maillard Reaction*, page 19 for more information). Most of the differences in flavor between one type of meat and another come from its fat: pork fat gives pork its taste and aroma, duck fat gives duck its flavor, etc. This is one of the reasons why well-marbled beef is so highly prized and why today's leaner pork and chicken are so bland.

The browning of lean tissues starts at around 265°F (130°C) and is what gives meat, poultry, and fish its savory, roasted, and broiled flavors. Because most sous vide cooking is done between 130°F (55°C) and 185°F (85°C), these savory and roasted flavors cannot develop. To give sous vide meat, poultry, and fish these flavors, you'll need to brown the surface after cooking. But to keep your perfectly cooked meat and poultry from overcooking when you sear it, you'll need to brown the surface as quickly as possible.

The fastest way to brown the surface without overcooking the interior is to sear it at a very high temperature for a very short time. The three most common ways to quickly sear meat and poultry are: in a heavy skillet with just smoking oil, on a very hot grill, or with a butane blowtorch.

This is the third tenet of sous vide cooking: *sear meat and poultry at a very high temperature for a very short time to develop meaty, savory, and roasted flavors.*

In addition to providing the flavors you expect in meat and poultry dishes, searing the meat for a very short time produces significantly fewer of the potentially carcinogenic chemical compounds, collectively called mutagens, compared with traditional cooking methods. So, by cooking meat and poultry sous vide and then searing them for a short time at a very high temperature, you retain more nutrients and produce fewer carcinogens than traditional cooking methods.

Learn by Doing: Chicken Breasts

Everyone has been served a dry and stringy chicken breast. Like fish, chicken breasts are only moist and tender if the highest temperature they reach is 140–145°F (60–62.5°C). Indeed, chicken breasts cooked to over about 150°F (65°C) will taste dry because the muscle fibers in the breast have shrunk (lengthwise) and squeezed out a substantial amount of water. (For more information on what happens to meat and poultry when it's heated, see *Science: The Effects of Heat on Meat*, page 20.)

Since poultry meat often contains harmful food pathogens, you'll need to be certain that you pasteurize the chicken breasts to make them safe to eat. With your precision water bath, you can easily hold the chicken breasts at 140°F (60°C) until they're pasteurized. It takes longer to pasteurize chicken at 140°F (60°C) than it does to pasteurize fish—see the food safety chapter on page 252 for more information.

Preheat your water bath to 140°F (60°C). Vacuum-seal a thawed, boneless, skinless chicken breast in a plastic pouch. Put the sealed pouch into the preheated water bath and cook it for at least 2 hours (and preferably less than 4 hours). Remove the chicken breast from the pouch and pat it dry with paper towels. Pour just enough high-smoke-point oil (such as grapeseed, peanut, or vegetable oil) into a heavy skillet to cover the bottom. Heat the oil over high heat, watching carefully, until it just begins to smoke. Put the chicken breast into the skillet and sear only one side until it's golden brown, about 15–25 seconds. Remove the chicken breast from the skillet and season it with salt and pepper.

You will find the chicken breast is moist, tender, and has a deep chicken flavor. How deep the chicken flavor is depends on the quality of the chicken you bought—many people find organic and free-range chickens have a more pronounced chicken flavor than caged chickens. Although cooking sous vide will bring out the best of any piece of meat, for the best results you should buy the highest quality meat you can afford.

Prolonged cooking has been used since ancient times to make tougher cuts of meat more palatable. In traditional braising, the meat simmers in liquid for several hours until it's fall-off-the-bone tender. This tenderizing occurs mostly from collagen's dissolving into gelatin and from the inter-fiber connections being reduced to essentially nothing. You can reproduce the taste and texture of a traditional braise by vacuum-sealing your meat and cooking it in a 175°F (80°C) water bath for 8–12 hours or in a 160°F (70°C) water bath for about a day.

With your precision water bath, you can also tenderize tougher, usually less expensive, cuts of meat at 130–140°F (55–60°C). Since doneness only depends on the highest temperature the meat reaches, you can cook a tough cut of meat for several days at 130°F (55°C) and it will be both fork tender and medium-rare! Most of the tenderizing at 130–140°F (55–60°C) occurs within the first 6 hours.

This is the fourth tenet of sous vide cooking: *transform tough cuts of meat into tender cuts by cooking them at 130–140°F (55–60°C) for 6–72 hours.*

Learn by Doing: Beef Chuck Roast

Some cuts of meat are tougher than others. Muscles that the animal uses a lot have more connective tissue (mostly collagen) and so are tougher. Consequently, cuts from the leg and shoulder of beef, pork, and lamb are tougher than cuts from the rib and back. With your precision water bath, you can transform these tough cuts into tender cuts by cooking them for extended periods at 130–140°F (55–60°C).

Preheat your water bath to 130°F (55°C) for a medium-rare roast or 140°F (60°C) for a medium roast. Vacuum-seal a chuck roast in a large pouch. Put the sealed pouch into the preheated water bath and cook it for 1 full day (24 hours). It's normal for the meat to have a slightly greenish-brown color and for the liquid in the pouch to be reddish. Remove the roast from the pouch and pat it dry with paper towels. Pour just enough high-smoke-point oil (such as grapeseed, peanut, or vegetable oil) into a heavy skillet to cover the bottom. Heat the oil over high heat, watching carefully, until it just begins to smoke. Sear each side of the roast until it is a deep mahogany brown, about 30–60 seconds per side. Remove the roast from the skillet and serve immediately.

You will find that the roast has a deep beefy flavor, is pink from edge-to-edge, and is as tender as a prime rib roast.

Brining has become increasingly popular in recent years and is now frequently used when cooking pork and poultry. Brining is not necessary when meat is cooked at its ideal temperature, but is useful when using sous vide to recreate traditional-style braises—say, for pulled pork or duck leg confit. Meat and poultry is brined by placing it into a 3 to 10% salt-water solution (2–6 tablespoons table salt per quart or 30–110 g salt per liter) for a few hours or even up to a few days. The brined meat is then rinsed under cold running water to remove excess salt and cooked as usual. Brining has two effects: it dissolves some of the support structure of the muscle fibers, so they don't squeeze out as much water when heated, and allows the meat to absorb between 10 and 25% of its weight in water (which may include aromatics from herbs and spices). While the meat will still lose around 20% of its weight when heated to above about 150°F (65°C), the net effect will be a loss of only about 0–12% of its original weight.

Learn by Doing: Pulled or Chopped Pork Shoulder

Pork shoulder (also known as Boston butt) is an inexpensive cut of meat with great flavor. To keep the meat moist and give it a smoky flavor, brine it in a mixture of kosher (or sea) salt and smoked salt before cooking it sous vide. To make the brine, in a large container stir 1 cup (200 g) Morton's kosher salt (or ⅔ cup table salt or 1⅓ cups Diamond Crystal kosher salt) and ½ cup (100 g) smoked salt into 1 gallon (4 liters) cold water until the salt has completely dissolved. Then cut the pork shoulder into 1½–2 inch (4–5 cm) slices, put them into the brine, cover the container, and refrigerate for ½–2 days (12–48 hours).

Preheat the water bath to 160°F (70°C). Meanwhile, rinse the pieces of pork under cold running water to remove excess salt. Vacuum-seal each piece of pork in a separate pouch. Put the sealed pouches into the water bath and cook them for 1 full day (24 hours). It's important that the pouches aren't tightly arranged or overlapping, as doing so may result in uneven or incomplete cooking. Unless your water bath has a rack to separate the pouches, you may need to cook the pork in two (or more) batches. When cooking the pork in batches, be sure to refrigerate or freeze the brined and vacuum-sealed pork until you're able to cook it.

When the pork has finished cooking, remove the pouches from the water bath and let them cool on the counter for about 15 minutes. Then remove the pork from the pouches and either pull or chop it into bite-size pieces. Top it with your favorite barbecue sauce and serve immediately.

You will find that the pork is exceptionally moist and tender with a light smoky flavor. I have little doubt that you'll find it to be the most delicious barbecued pork you have ever eaten.

Science: The Maillard Reaction

The Maillard or browning reaction is a very complex reaction between amino acids and reducing sugars. After the initial reaction, an unstable inter-mediate structure is formed that undergoes further changes and produces hundreds of reaction by-products.

The Maillard reaction can be increased: by adding a reducing sugar, such as glucose, fructose, or lactose; by increasing the pH with a pinch of baking soda; or by increasing the temperature. Even small increases in pH greatly enhance the Maillard reaction and result in sweeter, nuttier, and more roasted-meat-like aromas. The addition of a little glucose—e.g., corn syrup—will also increase the Maillard reaction and improve the flavor pro-file. The Maillard reaction occurs noticeably around 265°F (130°C), but produces a boiled rather than a roasted aroma; good browning and a roasted flavor can be achieved at temperatures around 300°F (150°C) with the addition of glucose. Yet, in order to limit overcooking, foods cooked sous vide are either browned at temperatures over 400°F (200°C) or brushed with a glucose wash and browned in a skillet at around 350°F (175°C). Because of the very short searing time, the production of mutagens (heterocyclic amines) that may be carcinogenic is unlikely to be significant.

Science: The Effects of Heat on Meat

Muscle meat is roughly 75% water, 20% protein, and 5% fat and other substances. The protein in meat can be divided into three groups: myofibrillar (50–55%), sarcoplasmic (30–34%), and connective tissue (10–15%). The myofibrillar proteins (mostly myosin and actin) and the connective tissue proteins (mostly collagen) contract when heated, while the sarcoplasmic proteins expand when heated.

During heating, the muscle fibers shrink transversely and longitudinally, the sarcoplasmic proteins aggregate and gel, and connective tissues shrink and solubilize. The muscle fibers begin to shrink at 95–105°F (35–40°C) and shrinkage increases almost linearly with temperature up to 175°F (80°C). The aggregation and gelation of sarcoplasmic proteins begins around 105°F (40°C) and finishes around 140°F (60°C). Connective tissues start shrinking around 140°F (60°C) but contract more intensely over 150°F (65°C).

The water-holding capacity of whole muscle meat is governed by the shrinking and swelling of myofibrils. Around 80% of the water in muscle meat is held within the myofibrils between the thick (myosin) and thin (actin) filaments. Between 105°F and 140°F (40°C and 60°C), the muscle fibers shrink transversely and widen the gap between fibers. Then, above 140°F–150°F (60°C–65°C) the muscle fibers shrink longitudinally and cause substantial water loss; the extent of this contraction increases with temperature.

Above its shrinking temperature collagen loses its structure, is soluble in water, and is called gelatin. While the peak temperature of denaturation of intact collagen is 144–145°F (62–63°C) [in fish, the shrinking temperature is 113°F/45°C], enzymatic denaturation by collagenase peaks at 131–135°F (55–57°C) and takes only about six hours to significantly tenderize the meat. While most the tenderizing occurs within about 24 hours at 130–140°F (55–60°C), the meat will become slightly more tender if cooked for 2–3 days (48–72 hours).

The Basics of Cooking Vegetables

Fresh raw vegetables are crisp in texture and are frequently cooked to make them tender. Ideally, vegetables should be cooked until they're easy to bite or chew but not until they're mushy—unless, of course, you want to prepare a soft, smooth purée. The increase in tenderness during cooking comes from the dissolving of the cementing material, pectin, that holds the cells in the vegetable together. In vegetables, this cementing material starts to dissolve around 180–185°F (82–85°C) and takes about three times longer at that temperature than it does in boiling water (212°F/100°C).

This is the fifth tenet of sous vide cooking: *cook non-starchy vegetables in a 185°F (85°C) water bath until they're just tender.*

Learn by Doing: Carrots

Preheat your water bath to 185°F (85°C). While the water bath is heating, vacuum-seal 1 cup (250 ml/125 g) baby carrots or peeled and sliced mature carrots, 2 tablespoon (30 ml/28 g) butter, and a pinch of salt and pepper in a pouch. When vacuum-sealing, try to keep the carrots in a single layer. Put the sealed pouch into the preheated water bath and cook it for 30–50 minutes.

You will find the carrots have great texture and a sweet, mild flavor. Moreover, vegetables that are cooked sous vide retain significantly more nutrients than vegetables that are steamed, boiled, microwaved, or baked.

The change in texture from cooking starchy vegetables (such as potatoes, sweet potatoes, winter squash, and corn) comes from both the dissolving of cementing material and the gelatinization of starch granules within their cells. The gelatinization of starch is what thickens sauces, soups, and stews. Since most starches gelatinize between 140–175°F (60–80°C), you can cook starchy vegetables in a 175°F (80°C) water bath for about twice as long as if you had boiled them.

Learn by Doing: Potatoes

Preheat the water bath to 175°F (80°C). While the water bath comes up to temperature, carefully wash a couple potatoes and, if desired, remove their skin. Cut the potatoes into bite-size pieces, toss them with extra virgin olive oil, and generously season them with salt and pepper. Vacuum-seal the potato pieces in one or more pouches so that they're in a single layer. Put the sealed pouch(es) into the preheated water bath and cook them for 1–1½ hours.

In this chapter you have learned that doneness only depends on temperature. You've learned that sous vide cooking gives you unparalleled control over safety and texture: that tough meat can be made tender and food pasteurized at 130°F (54.5°C) or above. You've learned how searing sous vide meat at a very high temperature for a very short time keeps it juicy and gives it great flavor. And you've learned how to cook vegetables sous vide.

Temperatures & Times *See note on page 31.*

Beef

Loin

Tenderloin steak

Rare, unpasteurized	125°F (50°C)	1–1½ hours
Medium-rare, unpasteurized	130°F (55°C)	1–1½ hours
Medium-rare	130°F (55°C)	2–2½ hours
Medium	140°F (60°C)	1–1½ hours

Tenderloin roast

Rare, unpasteurized	125°F (50°C)	1½–2 hours
Medium-rare, unpasteurized	130°F (55°C)	1½–2 hours
Medium-rare	130°F (55°C)	2½–3 hours
Medium	140°F (60°C)	1½–2 hours

Top loin (strip) steak

Rare, unpasteurized	125°F (50°C)	1–1½ hours
Medium-rare, unpasteurized	130°F (55°C)	1–1½ hours
Medium-rare	130°F (55°C)	2–2½ hours
Medium	140°F (60°C)	1–1½ hours

Top loin (strip) roast

Rare, unpasteurized	125°F (50°C)	2–3 hours
Medium-rare, unpasteurized	130°F (55°C)	2–3 hours
Medium-rare	130°F (55°C)	3–4 hours
Medium	140°F (60°C)	2–3 hours

Porterhouse or T-bone steak

Rare, unpasteurized	125°F (50°C)	1–1½ hours
Medium-rare, unpasteurized	130°F (55°C)	1–1½ hours
Medium-rare	130°F (55°C)	2–2½ hours
Medium	140°F (60°C)	1–1½ hours

Rib

Rib or rib-eye steak

Rare, unpasteurized	125°F (50°C)	1–1½ hours
Medium-rare	130°F (55°C)	6–8 hours
Medium	140°F (60°C)	6–8 hours

Rib-eye or prime rib roast

Rare, unpasteurized	125°F (50°C)	3–4 hours
Medium-rare	130°F (55°C)	8–12 hours
Medium	140°F (60°C)	8–12 hours

Sirloin

Tri-tip or sirloin tip steak

Medium-rare	130°F (55°C)	6–8 hours
Medium	140°F (60°C)	6–8 hours

Tri-tip roast

Medium-rare	130°F (55°C)	8–12 hours
Medium	140°F (60°C)	8–12 hours

Top sirloin steak

Medium-rare	130°F (55°C)	1–2 days (24–48 hours)
Medium	140°F (60°C)	1–2 days (24–48 hours)

Chuck

Flat-iron or top blade steak

Rare, unpasteurized	125°F (50°C)	1–1½ hours
Medium-rare	130°F (55°C)	6–8 hours
Medium	140°F (60°C)	6–8 hours

Shoulder or ranch steak

Medium-rare	130°F (55°C)	6–8 hours
Medium	140°F (60°C)	6–8 hours

Short ribs

Medium-rare	130°F (55°C)	1–2 days (24–48 hours)
Medium	140°F (60°C)	1–2 days (24 48 hours)
Well, slow	160°F (70°C)	1 day (24 hours)
Well, quick	175°F (80°C)	10–14 hours

Chuck roast

Medium-rare	130°F (55°C)	1–2 days (24–48 hours)
Medium	140°F (60°C)	1–2 days (24–48 hours)
Well, slow	160°F (70°C)	1 day (24 hours)
Well, quick	175°F (80°C)	10 14 hours

Chuck 7-bone steak

Medium-rare	130°F (55°C)	1–2 days (24–48 hours)
Medium	140°F (60°C)	1–2 days (24–48 hours)
Well, slow	160°F (70°C)	1 day (24 hours)
Well, quick	175°F (80°C)	10–14 hours

Chuck eye steak, boneless

Medium-rare	130°F (55°C)	2–3 days (48–72 hours)
Medium	140°F (60°C)	2–3 days (48–72 hours)
Well, slow	160°F (70°C)	1–2 days (24–48 hours)
Well, quick	175°F (80°C)	12–24 hours

Round

Top round steak

Medium-rare	130°F (55°C)	1–2 days (24–48 hours)
Medium	140°F (60°C)	1–2 days (24–48 hours)
Well, slow	160°F (70°C)	1 day (24 hours)
Well, quick	175°F (80°C)	10–14 hours

Eye round steak

Medium-rare	130°F (55°C)	1–2 days (24–48 hours)
Medium	140°F (60°C)	1–2 days (24–48 hours)
Well, slow	160°F (70°C)	1 day (24 hours)
Well, quick	175°F (80°C)	10–14 hours

Bottom round steak

Medium-rare	130°F (55°C)	2–3 days (48–72 hours)
Medium	140°F (60°C)	2–3 days (48–72 hours)
Well, slow	160°F (70°C)	1–2 days (24–48 hours)
Well, quick	175°F (80°C)	12–24 hours

Round roast

Medium-rare	130°F (55°C)	2–3 days (48–72 hours)
Medium	140°F (60°C)	2–3 days (48–72 hours)
Well, slow	160°F (70°C)	1–2 days (24–48 hours)
Well, quick	175°F (80°C)	12–24 hours

Other

Brisket

Medium-rare	130°F (55°C)	2–3 days (48–72 hours)
Medium	140°F (60°C)	2–3 days (48–72 hours)
Well, slow	160°F (70°C)	1–2 days (24–48 hours)
Well, quick	175°F (80°C)	12–24 hours

Cheek

Medium-rare	130°F (55°C)	2–3 days (48–72 hours)
Medium	140°F (60°C)	2–3 days (48–72 hours)
Well, slow	160°F (70°C)	1–2 days (24–48 hours)
Well, quick	175°F (80°C)	12–24 hours

Flank steak

Medium-rare	130°F (55°C)	1–2 days (24–48 hours)
Medium	140°F (60°C)	1–2 days (24–48 hours)
Well, slow	160°F (70°C)	1 day (24 hours)
Well, quick	175°F (80°C)	10–14 hours

Shank

Medium-rare	130°F (55°C)	2–3 days (48–72 hours)
Medium	140°F (60°C)	2–3 days (48–72 hours)
Well, slow	160°F (70°C)	1–2 days (24–48 hours)
Well, quick	175°F (80°C)	12–24 hours

Skirt steak

Medium-rare	130°F (55°C)	1–2 days (24–48 hours)
Medium	140°F (60°C)	1–2 days (24–48 hours)
Well, slow	160°F (70°C)	1 day (24 hours)
Well, quick	175°F (80°C)	10–14 hours

Hamburger, less than 1 inch (25 mm) thick

Medium-rare	130°F (55°C)	2–2½ hours
Medium	140°F (60°C)	1–1½ hours

Pork

Loin

Tenderloin

Medium-rare	130°F (55°C)	3–4 hours
Medium	140°F (60°C)	2–3 hours

Loin chops

Medium-rare	130°F (55°C)	2½–3½ hours
Medium	140°F (60°C)	1½–2½ hours

Loin roast

Medium-rare	130°F (55°C)	4–5 hours
Medium	140°F (60°C)	3½–4½ hours

Rib chops or roast

Medium-rare	130°F (55°C)	6–8 hours
Medium	140°F (60°C)	6–8 hours

Sirloin chops or roast

Medium-rare	130°F (55°C)	8–12 hours
Medium	140°F (60°C)	8–12 hours

Back and country-style ribs

Medium-rare	130°F (55°C)	8–12 hours
Medium	140°F (60°C)	8–12 hours
Well, slow	160°F (70°C)	8–12 hours
Well, quick	175°F (80°C)	6–8 hours

Shoulder

Boston butt

Medium-rare	130°F (55°C)	1–2 days (24–48 hours)
Medium	140°F (60°C)	1–2 days (24–48 hours)
Well, slow	160°F (70°C)	1 day (24 hours)
Well, quick	175°F (80°C)	8–12 hours

Blade steak

Medium-rare	130°F (55°C)	1–2 days (24–48 hours)
Medium	140°F (60°C)	1–2 days (24–48 hours)

Picnic roast

Medium-rare	130°F (55°C)	2–3 days (48–72 hours)
Medium	140°F (60°C)	2–3 days (48–72 hours)
Well, slow	160°F (70°C)	1–2 days (24–48 hours)
Well, quick	175°F (80°C)	12–24 hours

Arm steak

Medium-rare	130°F (55°C)	2–3 days (48–72 hours)
Medium	140°F (60°C)	2–3 days (48–72 hours)

Ham or Leg

Ham, slice (½–¾ inch/15–20 mm thick)

Medium-rare	130°F (55°C)	1½–2½ hours
Medium	140°F (60°C)	1–2 hours

Ham, shank or butt portion

Medium-rare	130°F (55°C)	7–9 hours
Medium	140°F (60°C)	5½–7 hours

Other

Spareribs

Well, slow	160°F (70°C)	1 day (24 hours)
Well, quick	175°F (80°C)	8–12 hours

Belly

Well, slow	160°F (70°C)	1 day (24 hours)
Well, quick	175°F (80°C)	8–12 hours

Lamb

Rack

Rack, trimmed

Rare, unpasteurized	125°F (50°C)	1–1½ hours
Medium-rare	130°F (55°C)	2½–3 hours
Medium	140°F (60°C)	1½–2 hours

Rib chop

Rare, unpasteurized	125°F (50°C)	1–1½ hours
Medium-rare	130°F (55°C)	2–2½ hours
Medium	140°F (60°C)	1½–2 hours

Loin

Tenderloin

Rare, unpasteurized	125°F (50°C)	1–1½ hours
Medium-rare	130°F (55°C)	2½–3 hours
Medium	140°F (60°C)	1½–2 hours

Loin roast

Rare, unpasteurized	125°F (50°C)	2–2½ hours
Medium-rare	130°F (55°C)	3–3¼ hours
Medium	140°F (60°C)	2–2½ hours

Loin, boneless

Rare, unpasteurized	125°F (50°C)	1–1½ hours
Medium-rare	130°F (55°C)	2½–3 hours
Medium	140°F (60°C)	1½–2 hours

Loin chops

Rare, unpasteurized	125°F (50°C)	1–1½ hours
Medium-rare	130°F (55°C)	2½–3 hours
Medium	140°F (60°C)	1½–2 hours

Sirloin steak

Medium-rare	130°F (55°C)	6–8 hours
Medium	140°F (60°C)	6–8 hours

Leg

Leg, boneless

Medium-rare	130°F (55°C)	1 day (24 hours)
Medium	140°F (60°C)	1 day (24 hours)

Leg steaks

| Medium-rare | 130°F (55°C) | 1 day (24 hours) |
| Medium | 140°F (60°C) | 1 day (24 hours) |

Top round

| Medium-rare | 130°F (55°C) | 1 day (24 hours) |
| Medium | 140°F (60°C) | 1 day (24 hours) |

Eye round

| Medium-rare | 130°F (55°C) | 1–2 days (24–48 hours) |
| Medium | 140°F (60°C) | 1–2 days (24–48 hours) |

Bottom round

| Medium-rare | 130°F (55°C) | 1–2 days (24–48 hours) |
| Medium | 140°F (60°C) | 1–2 days (24–48 hours) |

Shank

Medium-rare	130°F (55°C)	2–3 days (48–72 hours)
Medium	140°F (60°C)	2–3 days (48–72 hours)
Well, slow	160°F (70°C)	1–2 days (24–48 hours)
Well, quick	175°F (80°C)	12–24 hours

Shoulder

Shoulder or square-cut chuck

Medium-rare	130°F (55°C)	1–2 days (24–48 hours)
Medium	140°F (60°C)	1–2 days (24–48 hours)
Well, slow	160°F (70°C)	1 day (24 hours)
Well, quick	175°F (80°C)	8–12 hours

Neck

Medium-rare	130°F (55°C)	2–3 days (48–72 hours)
Medium	140°F (60°C)	2–3 days (48–72 hours)
Well, slow	160°F (70°C)	1–2 days (24–48 hours)
Well, quick	175°F (80°C)	12–24 hours

Other

Arm chop

| Medium-rare | 130°F (55°C) | 1–2 days (24–48 hours) |
| Medium | .140°F (60°C) | 1–2 days (24–48 hours) |

Blade chop

| Medium-rare | 130°F (55°C) | 1 day (24 hours) |
| Medium | 140°F (60°C) | 1 day (24 hours) |

Breast or ribs

Well, slow	160°F (70°C)	1 day (24 hours)
Well, quick	175°F (80°C)	8–12 hours

Foreshank or breast shank

Medium-rare	130°F (55°C)	2–3 days (48–72 hours)
Medium	140°F (60°C)	2–3 days (48–72 hours)
Well, slow	160°F (70°C)	1–2 days (24–48 hours)
Well, quick	175°F (80°C)	12–24 hours

Venison

Chuck or shoulder

Medium-rare	130°F (55°C)	1–2 days (24–48 hours)
Medium	140°F (60°C)	1–2 days (24–48 hours)

Rack or ribs

Rare, unpasteurized	125°F (50°C)	1–1½ hours
Medium-rare	130°F (55°C)	6–8 hours
Medium	140°F (60°C)	6–8 hours

Loin

Rare, unpasteurized	125°F (50°C)	1–1½ hours
Medium-rare, unpasteurized	130°F (55°C)	1–1½ hours
Medium-rare	130°F (55°C)	2–2½ hours
Medium	140°F (60°C)	1–1½ hours

Hip

Medium-rare	130°F (55°C)	12–18 hours
Medium	140°F (60°C)	12–18 hours

Leg

Medium-rare	130°F (55°C)	1–2 days (24–48 hours)
Medium	140°F (60°C)	1–2 days (24–48 hours)

Eggs & Poultry

Chicken

Breast

Medium	140°F (60°C)	2–3 hours

Leg, thigh or drumstick

Well, slow	160°F (70°C)	8–12 hours
Well, quick	175°F (80°C)	4–6 hours

Eggs

Soft-boiled	148°F (64.5°C)	45–60 minutes
Hard-boiled	167°F (75°C)	45–60 minutes
Pasteurized	135°F (57°C)	75 minutes

Turkey

Breast

Medium	140°F (60°C)	2 ½–3 ½ hours

Leg, thigh or drumstick

Well, slow	160°F (70°C)	1 day (24 hours)
Well, quick	175°F (80°C)	8–12 hours

Duck

Breast

Medium-rare	135°F (57°C)	2 ½–3 ½ hours

Leg, thigh or drumstick

Well, slow	160°F (70°C)	1 day (24 hours)
Well, quick	175°F (80°C)	8–12 hours

Fish & Shellfish

Fish, cut into individual portions

Rare, unpasteurized	108°F (42°C)	15–20 minutes
Medium-rare, unpasteurized	122°F (50°C)	15–20 minutes
Medium	140°F (60°C)	40–50 minutes

Shellfish

Rare, unpasteurized	108°F (42°C)	15–20 minutes
Medium-rare, unpasteurized	122°F (50°C)	15–20 minutes
Medium	140°F (60°C)	30–40 minutes

Vegetables, Fruits & Legumes

Cabbage family

Broccoli (Blanched)	185°F (85°C)	25–35 minutes
Brussels sprouts	185°F (85°C)	45–60 minutes
Cabbage	185°F (85°C)	30–45 minutes
Cauliflower	185°F (85°C)	30–40 minutes

Soft-shell squash

Summer squash	185°F (85°C)	45–60 minutes
Zucchini	185°F (85°C)	45–60 minutes

Hard-shell squash

Acorn or butternut squash	175°F (80°C)	2–2 ¼ hours

Pumpkin	175°F (80°C)	1–1½ hours
Onion family		
Leeks	185°F (85°C)	45–60 minutes
Onions	185°F (85°C)	1–1½ hours
Pod and seed vegetables		
Green Beans (Blanched)	185°F (85°C)	45–60 minutes
Corn	185°F (85°C)	30–45 minutes
Fresh Peas	175°F (80°C)	30–40 minutes
Root vegetables		
Beets	185°F (85°C)	1–1½ hours
Carrots	185°F (85°C)	30–50 minutes
Celery Root	185°F (85°C)	1–1½ hours
Parsnips	185°F (85°C)	30–45 minutes
Rutabagas	185°F (85°C)	2–2½ hours
Turnips	185°F (85°C)	30–60 minutes
Tubers		
Potatoes	175°F (80°C)	1–1½ hours
Sweet Potatoes	175°F (80°C)	1–1½ hours
Shoots and stalks		
Artichokes	185°F (85°C)	1½–2 hours
Asparagus	185°F (85°C)	45–60 minutes
Fruits		
Apples	185°F (85°C)	30–40 minutes
Pears	185°F (85°C)	25–35 minutes
Dried Beans		
Black beans	195°F (90°C)	3½–4½ hours
Cranberry beans	195°F (90°C)	2½–3½ hours
Chickpeas or garbanzo beans	195°F (90°C)	5–6 hours
Great northern beans	195°F (90°C)	3–4 hours
Kidney beans	195°F (90°C)	3–4 hours
Lentils beans	195°F (90°C)	¾–1 hours
Navy or Yankee beans	195°F (90°C)	2½–3½ hours
Pinto beans	195°F (90°C)	4–5 hours

Note: Any time in the range given should give excellent results. Up to double the time will usually give acceptable results if your schedule requires it. This book assumes you got your ingredients from a supermarket; exceptional ingredients, like Kobe-style beef, may need less time; occasionally you may get meat that remains tough regardless of cooking time (see page 34).

Meat

Meat has been an important part of our diets for 100,000 years, and we have raised animals for food for at least 9,000 years. The last few decades, however, have seen dramatic changes in the meat we eat. Today's meat is from younger and leaner animals, which may have traveled halfway across the world to reach our tables. Since traditional cooking methods weren't designed for today's leaner and younger meat, they often produce dry and flavorless results. Thankfully, sous vide cooking allows us to cook almost any cut of meat so that it's moist, tender and flavorful.

Tenderness & Time

Tenderness is very highly prized—the tenderest cut of beef, the tenderloin, is also the most expensive cut of beef. The toughness of meat comes from an abundance of connective tissue.[1] With sous vide cooking, we can transform tough cuts into tender cuts by converting this tough collagen into soft gelatin.

Muscles that are well worked have connective tissue that makes them tougher than muscles that were exercised comparatively little or that are from young animals. That's why cuts from the chuck and round are tougher than cuts from the rib and loin. Likewise, cuts from the lower half of the animal are tougher than cuts from the upper half: cuts from the chuck are tenderer than cuts from the brisket.

Cooking can convert a significant amount of this tough collagen into soft gelatin, and so transform a tough cut of meat into a tender cut. How long this conversion takes depends on the cooking temperature: tough cuts of meat, like beef chuck and pork shoulder, take 10–12 hours at 175°F (80°C) or 1–2 days (24–48 hours) at 130–140°F (55–60°C) to become fork-tender. At cooking temperatures between 130°F (55°C) and about 140°F (60°C), an enzyme in the meat called collagenase can convert some of the collagen into gelatin and significantly increase the tenderness of the meat in about six hours. This is why intermediate cuts of meat, like beef sirloin, only needs 6–8 hours at 130–140°F (55–60°C) to become deliciously tender.

---

[1] Connective tissue is mostly the proteins, collagen and elastin. We are very fortunate that most muscles have very little elastin, which is rubber-like and doesn't soften during cooking. Meat that should be tender because it has little connective tissue, however, can be made very tough by something called cold-shortenings or actomyosin toughness. Actomyosin toughness occurs when muscles are allowed to contract (shorten) during the onset of rigor mortis. Unfortunately, there is no way for you to determine at the market if the meat was mishandled during slaughter and allowed to shorten.

Doneness & Temperature

The doneness of meat is determined by the highest temperature it reaches: 125°F (50°C) is rare, 130°F (55°C) is medium-rare, 140°F (60°C) is medium, and 160°F (70°C) and above is well done. The beauty of sous vide cooking is that you just set the water bath to your desired degree of doneness and then choose the cooking time based on your desired tenderness.

While two similar cuts cooked to the same internal temperature will have a similar plumpness and juiciness, their color may be different. The color of meat cooked to the same temperature depends on how quickly it reaches that temperature and on how long it's held at that temperature: the faster it comes up to temperature, the redder it is; the longer it's held at a particular temperature, the paler it becomes. In other words, a tougher cut of meat that's cooked at 130°F (55°C) for a day will have the taste and texture of a tender cut of meat cooked medium-rare, but may look as if it was cooked medium.

Searing

The meaty, savory, and roasted flavors in meat come from the browning of its lean tissues, a process called the Maillard reaction. Like the conversion of collagen into gelatin, the Maillard reaction occurs much faster at higher temperatures; while it takes less than a minute to brown meat in a 400°F (200°C) skillet, it would take 4 weeks in a 140°F (60°C) water bath! To prevent your perfectly cooked meat from overcooking, you'll need to sear the surface as quickly as possible. The three most common ways to quickly sear meat are: in a heavy skillet with just smoking oil, on a very hot grill, and with a blowtorch.

When searing meat on the cooktop, you'll want to use a high-smoke-point oil and a heavy skillet. A high-smoke-point oil (such as grapeseed, peanut, or vegetable oil) can be heated to at least 400°F (200°C) before it starts to break down. A heavy skillet—such as a stainless steel skillet with a thick aluminum-clad bottom or a cast iron skillet—will retain its heat when the cooler meat comes into contact with the hot metal and won't warp with repeated use. A smoking-hot skillet works particularly well, because the oil evenly distributes the heat over the surface of the meat. It's important that you use just enough oil to coat the bottom of the skillet, otherwise the surface of the meat will brown unevenly and may burn in spots.

Browning meat on a very hot grill or under the broiler (salamander) is also a great solution. It's important that you get the grill or broiler as hot as possible and sear only one side at a time—which is in contrast with cooking raw meat on a grill, where you should flip the meat every 30–60 seconds until the core reaches your desired temperature.

A blowtorch gives the most control and is great for searing beef, lamb, and venison. Blowtorches tend to burn pork, poultry, and fish, so be careful there. The butane kitchen blowtorch from Iwatani works very well for searing meat (and crème brulée). Plumbing propane blowtorches are easy to find, but can leave an off-flavor. Using the blowtorch through a fine-mesh wire chinois will eliminate this off-flavor, but may damage your chinois. To sear the meat with a blowtorch, hold it 4–6 inches (10–15 cm) from the surface of the meat and move the flame in small circles over the surface of the beef, lamb, or venison until it's mahogany brown in color.

Food Safety & Pasteurization

The interior of intact steaks, chops, and roasts is generally considered to be sterile, and is the reason that most traditional cooking methods don't pasteurize steaks or roasts. But many processors are now mechanically tenderizing the meat before it reaches your local market using hundreds of blades or needles that can push food pathogens from the surface of the meat into the interior. This mechanically tenderized meat looks like intact meat and may not be labeled as being mechanically tenderized. Unfortunately, mechanically tenderized meat must be pasteurized in order to make it safe to eat. Therefore, I recommended that you pasteurize all the meat you cook.

Grilled Loin or Rib Steak

Makes 4 Servings

4 (10 ounce/280 g) tenderloin, top loin (strip), rib-eye, or rib steaks; or 2 (20 ounce/560 g) thick-cut (1½–1¾ inches/40–45 mm thick), porterhouse, or T-bone steaks

Salt and black pepper

2–3 tablespoons (30–40 ml) vegetable oil (optional)

1. Preheat the water bath to 125°F (50°C) for a rare steak, 130°F (55°C) for a medium-rare steak, or 140°F (60°C) for a medium steak.

2. Vacuum-seal each steak in a separate pouch.

3. Put the sealed pouches into the preheated water bath. Cook tenderloin, top-loin (strip), porterhouse, and T-bone steaks for 1–1½ hours. Cook rib or rib-eye steaks for 1–1½ hours at 125°F (50°C) or for 6–8 hours at 130°F (55°C) or 140°F (60°C).

Pasteurization: When serving immune compromised individuals, cook a 1–1¼ inch (25–30 mm) thick, thawed steak for at least 2 hours at 130°F (55°C) or 1 hour at 140°F (60°C) to ensure that it's safe for them to eat. Note: Since rib and rib-eye steaks can be a bit tough, you can tenderize them by cooking them for 6–8 hours at 130–140°F (55–60°C). You cannot tenderize them this way at 125°F (50°C) because some food pathogens grow at this temperature.

4. About 15 minutes before serving, preheat a gas or charcoal grill until it's very hot.

5. Remove the steaks from the pouches and pat them dry with paper towels.

6. Lightly brush the steaks with oil and generously season them with salt and pepper.

7. Put the steaks on the very hot grill and sear each side until it's nicely browned, about one minute per side.

Alternative: The steaks can also be seared in a smoking-hot skillet.
1. Pour just enough high-smoke-point oil into a heavy skillet to cover the bottom. Heat the oil over high heat, watching carefully, until it just begins to smoke.
2. Sear each side of the steaks until it's a deep mahogany brown, about 15–25 seconds per side. Work in batches, if necessary, to avoid overcrowding the skillet.
3. After searing, blot the steaks with a paper towel to remove excess oil.

8. Serve immediately.

...with Choron Sauce

Makes 4 Servings

This sauce also goes well on chicken, duck, white fish, lamb, rabbit, salmon, shellfish, and turkey.

4 cooked loin or rib steaks, seared and warm (see recipe on page 37)

1 small shallot, peeled and finely chopped

1 tablespoon (15 ml) tarragon or white wine vinegar

¼ cup (60 ml) water

1 pinch ground black pepper

3 large egg yolks, pasteurized as on page 164

1 tablespoon (15 ml) tomato paste

12 tablespoons (175 ml/170 g) unsalted butter

Lemon juice to taste

Salt and black pepper to taste

1. Put the shallot, vinegar, water, and pepper into a small saucepan over high heat.

2. Bring the liquid to a boil and cook until the volume is reduced to 1½–2 tablespoons (25–30 ml).

3. Strain the mixture into a medium saucepan to remove the shallots.

4. Add the egg yolks and tomato paste to the vinegar mixture and stir until it's smooth.

5. Cut the butter into 12 pieces and add all the butter to the pan.

6. Put the saucepan over medium-low heat and whisk slowly until all the butter has melted.

7. Continue whisking the sauce until it just thickens (at around 160°F/70°C).

8. Remove the pan from the heat and season the sauce with lemon juice, salt, and pepper.

> *Alternative: You can also make this classic sauce sous vide.*
> *1. Preheat a water bath to 148°F (64.5°C).*
> *2. Put the strained vinegar mixture, egg yolks, tomato paste, and butter into a heat-stable, resealable pouch, squeeze out all the air, and seal.*
> *3. Put the sealed pouch into the preheated water bath. Remove the pouch, agitate the contents, and return it to the water bath every few minutes until the butter has completely melted. Then remove, agitate the*

contents, and replace the pouch every 5–10 minutes until the sauce has thickened, about 20–30 minutes of total cooking time.

4. Just before serving, remove the pouch from the water bath and season with lemon juice, salt, and pepper.

9. Spoon the sauce over the warm, seared steaks and serve immediately.

Variation: For a Béarnaise sauce, replace the tomato paste with 1 tablespoon (15 ml) chopped fresh tarragon leaves.

...with Parsley Butter

Makes 4 Servings

Compound butters, such as these, are also great on chicken, duck, white fish, lamb, pork, rabbit, salmon, shellfish, and venison.

4 cooked loin or rib steaks, seared and warm (see recipe on page 37)

8 tablespoons (125 ml/114 g) unsalted butter, softened

¼ cup (60 ml/15 g) chopped fresh parsley

1 clove (3 g) peeled garlic, minced or pressed

1 teaspoon (5 ml) lemon juice

1 teaspoon (5 ml/5 g) prepared Dijon-style mustard

Salt and black pepper to taste

1. Beat the butter until it's creamy.

2. Stir in the parsley, garlic, lemon juice, and mustard until smooth.

3. Form the butter into a log using plastic wrap and refrigerate until needed.

4. Top each warm, seared steak with a quarter of the flavored butter and serve immediately.

> *Variation: Replace the parsley with an equal amount of finely chopped fresh dill weed.*

> *Variation: Replace the parsley with an equal amount of finely chopped fresh basil and replace the lemon juice with an equal amount of balsamic vinegar.*

...with Tomato and Chipotle Sauce

Makes 4 Servings

This sauce also goes well on catfish, chicken, duck, white fish, lamb, pork, rabbit, salmon, and shellfish. For some variety, add a ¼ teaspoon (1 ml) ground coriander and a small zucchini cut into bite-size pieces after puréeing the tomato mixture.

4 cooked loin or rib steaks, seared and warm (see recipe on page 37)

1 can (14 ½ ounce/412 g) diced tomatoes, drained

2–3 canned chipotle chiles in adobo sauce, rinsed and chopped

2 cloves (6 g) peeled garlic, minced or pressed

2 tablespoon (30 ml) lard or vegetable oil

1 tablespoon (15 ml) chopped fresh cilantro

Salt and black pepper to taste

1. Put the tomatoes, chilies, and garlic into a food processor or blender and pulse until the tomato mixture is the consistency of a chunky puree.

2. In a saucepan, heat the lard (or oil) over medium-high heat until shimmering.

3. Add the tomato mixture (and the coriander and chunks of zucchini, if using) and cook, stirring constantly, until darkened and reduced to the desired consistency.

4. Reduce the heat to low, stir in the cilantro, and season with salt and pepper.

5. Spoon the sauce over the warm, seared steaks and serve immediately

Pan-Seared Sirloin Steak
Makes 4 Servings

4 (10 ounce/280 g) tri-tip or top sirloin steaks, boneless
Salt and black pepper to taste
High-smoke-point oil, such as grapeseed, peanut, or vegetable

1. Preheat the water bath to 130°F (55°C) for a medium-rare steak or 140°F (60°C) for a medium steak.

2. Vacuum-seal each steak in a separate pouch.

3. Put the sealed pouches into the water bath and cook tri-tip steaks for 6–8 hours or top sirloin steaks for 1–2 days (24–48 hours).

> *Freezing: You can freeze the cooked steaks for up to a year.*
> *1. Put the sealed pouches into an ice water bath that's at least half ice for about 30 minutes.*
> *2. Dry the pouches with a towel and put them into a freezer.*
> *3. To reheat the steaks, put the frozen pouches into a preheated 130°F (55°C) water bath for about 45 minutes.*

4. Remove the steaks from their pouches. A slightly greenish-brown color is normal and will disappear after searing.

5. Pat the steaks dry with paper towels and generously season them with salt and pepper.

6. Pour just enough oil into a heavy skillet to cover the bottom. Heat the oil over high heat, watching carefully, until it just begins to smoke.

7. Sear each side of the steaks until it's a deep mahogany brown, about 15–25 seconds per side. Work in batches, if necessary, to avoid over-crowding the skillet.

8. Remove the steaks from the skillet and blot them with a paper towel to remove excess oil.

> *Alternative: The steaks can also be finished on the grill.*
> *1. Preheat a gas or charcoal grill until it's very hot.*
> *2. Lightly oil the steaks and season them with salt and pepper.*
> *3. Put the steaks on the very hot grill and sear each side until it's mahogany brown, about one minute per side.*

9. Serve immediately.

Pan-Seared Sirloin Steak

...with Flavored Butter

Makes 4 Servings

This compound butter has many ingredients, but is well worth the effort.

4 cooked sirloin steaks, seared and warm (see recipe on page 42)

8 tablespoons (125 ml/114 g) unsalted butter, softened

1 teaspoon (5 ml/5 g) ketchup

½ teaspoon (2 ml) prepared Dijon-style mustard

1 clove (3 g) peeled garlic, minced or pressed

1 teaspoon (5 ml) anchovy paste or 1 canned anchovy fillet, rinsed and finely chopped

1 teaspoon (5 ml/3 g) small capers, drained

4 teaspoons (20 ml/14 g) peeled and chopped shallot

2 tablespoons (30 ml/8 g) chopped fresh parsley

1 tablespoon (15 ml/3 g) chopped fresh chives

½ teaspoon (2 ml) dried dill weed

½ teaspoon (2 ml) dried ground tarragon

¼ teaspoon (1 ml) ground white pepper

1 teaspoon (5 ml) lemon juice

1. In a bowl, use a mixer to beat the butter until it's lightened in color and is creamy.

2. In a separate bowl, stir the ketchup, mustard, garlic, anchovy, capers, shallots, parsley, chives, dill, tarragon, white pepper, and lemon juice until it's well mixed.

3. Stir or beat the herb mixture into the butter until it's smooth.

4. Top each warm, seared steak with a quarter of the flavored butter and serve immediately.

...with Horseradish Cream Sauce

Makes 4 Servings

This sauce also goes well on chicken, white fish, pork, salmon, shrimp, and venison.

4 cooked sirloin steaks, seared and warm (see recipe on page 42)

¾ cup (175 ml/173 g) sour cream

¼ cup (60 ml) heavy cream

2 teaspoons (10 ml/10 g) prepared horseradish

¼ cup (60 ml/12 g) chopped fresh chives

½ teaspoon (2 ml) prepared mustard

1 pinch granulated sugar

Salt and black pepper to taste

1. In a small bowl, stir together the sour cream, heavy cream, horseradish, chives, mustard, and sugar until smooth.

2. Season with salt and pepper.

3. Cover and refrigerate until needed.

4. Spoon the sauce over the warm, seared steaks and serve immediately.

Variation: Substitute the juice of 1 lime for the chives and mustard.

...with *Salsa Verde*

Makes 4 Servings

This salsa also goes well on chicken, duck, white fish, lamb, pork, rabbit, salmon, and shellfish.

4 cooked sirloin steaks, seared and warm (see recipe on page 42)

4 medium tomatillos, husked and rinsed, about 1½ cups (140 g) when chopped

2 fresh serrano chiles, about 1 tablespoon (12 g)

1 clove (3 g) garlic, peeled

1 small onion, peeled and finely chopped, about ½ cup (70 g)

¼ cup (60 ml/4 g) chopped fresh cilantro

2 tablespoons (30 ml) lard or vegetable oil

½ cup (125 ml) chicken stock

Salt and sugar to taste

1. Preheat a gas or charcoal grill until it's very hot.

2. Roast the tomatillos on the grill until they blister and soften. Set them on a plate to cool.

3. In a skillet over medium heat, roast the chiles and whole garlic clove until the peppers are blackened in spots.

4. Remove the garlic and peppers from the pan. Peel the blackened skins from the peppers. (For a milder salsa, remove the stem and seeds from the peppers.)

5. Put the tomatillos, peppers, garlic, onions, and cilantro into a food processor or blender and pulse until it's reduced to a coarse purée.

6. In a saucepan, heat the lard (or oil) over medium-high heat until shimmering.

7. Add the tomatillo mixture and cook until the sauce has darkened and thickened.

8. Add the stock and bring the sauce to a boil. Continue to cook, stirring occasionally, until the sauce has been reduced to your desired consistency.

9. Reduce the heat to low and season with salt and sugar.

10. Spoon the salsa over the warm, seared steaks and serve immediately.

Grilled Chuck or Round Steak
Makes 4 Servings

4 (10 ounce/280 g) flat-iron (top blade), shoulder (ranch), chuck 7-bone, chuck eye, top round, eye round, or bottom round steaks; or 8 (5 ounce/140 g) boneless short ribs

Salt and black pepper to taste

2–3 tablespoons (30–40 ml) vegetable oil (optional)

1. Preheat the water bath to 130°F (55°C) for a medium-rare steak or 140°F (60°C) for a medium steak.

2. Vacuum-seal each steak in a separate pouch.

3. Put the sealed pouches into the water bath and cook flat-iron (top blade) or shoulder (ranch) steaks for 6–8 hours; short ribs or chuck 7-bone, top round, or eye round steaks for 1–2 days (24–48 hours); or chuck eye or bottom round steaks for 2–3 days (48–72 hours).

> *Freezing: You can freeze the cooked steaks for up to a year.*
> *1. Put the sealed pouches into an ice water bath that's at least half ice for about 30 minutes.*
> *2. Dry the pouches off with a towel and put them into a freezer.*
> *3. To reheat the steaks, put the frozen pouches into a preheated 130°F (55°C) water bath for about 45 minutes.*

4. Preheat a gas or charcoal grill until it's very hot.

5. Remove the steaks from their pouches. A slight greenish-brown color is normal and will disappear after searing.

6. Pat the steaks dry with paper towels, lightly brush with oil, and generously season with salt and pepper.

7. Put the steaks on the very hot grill and sear each side until mahogany brown in color, about one minute per side.

> *Alternative: The steaks can also be pan-seared.*
> *1. Pat the steaks dry with paper towels and generously season with salt and pepper.*
> *2. Pour just enough high-smoke-point oil into a heavy skillet to cover the bottom. Heat the oil over high heat, watching carefully, until it just begins to smoke.*
> *3. Sear each side of the steaks until it's mahogany brown in color, about 15–25 seconds per side. Work in batches, if necessary, to avoid over-crowding the skillet.*
> *4. Remove the steaks from the pan and blot them with a paper towel to remove excess oil.*

8. Serve the steaks immediately.

Grilled Chuck or Round Steak
...with Creamy Mushroom Sauce
Makes 4 Servings

This sauce is also great on chicken, white fish, lamb, pork, rabbit, salmon, shellfish, and venison.

4 cooked chuck or round steaks, seared and warm
(see recipe on page 46)

3 tablespoons (45 ml/43 g) unsalted butter

8 ounces (225 g) fresh specialty mushrooms,[2] thinly sliced

1 small shallot, peeled and finely chopped

1 clove (3 g) peeled garlic, minced or pressed

1½ tablespoons (20 ml/12 g) flour

1 cup (250 ml) whole milk

1 teaspoons (5 ml) dried rosemary

1 teaspoon (5 ml/5 g) prepared Dijon-style mustard

Juice of 1 lemon, about 3 tablespoons (45 ml)

Salt and black pepper to taste

1. Melt the butter in a skillet over medium heat.

2. Add the mushrooms and shallot. Cook, stirring frequently, until both are tender and the shallot is translucent.

3. Add the garlic and continue to cook until it's golden brown and fragrant.

4. Stir in the flour and continue cooking until it smells toasty and turns a light brown.

5. Stir in the milk, rosemary, mustard, and lemon juice. Continue to cook, stirring frequently, until the sauce has thickened.

6. Reduce the heat to low and season with salt and pepper.

7. Spoon the sauce over the warm, seared steaks and serve immediately.

---

2 Good choices include: chanterelle, crimini, morel, portabella, and shiitake. If using shiitake mushrooms, discard the stems.

Grilled Chuck or Round Steak

...with Blue Cheese and Honey Sauce

Makes 4 Servings

This sauce is also great on lamb.

4 cooked chuck or round steaks, seared and warm (see recipe on page 46)

2 tablespoons (30 ml/30 g) mayonnaise

1 tablespoons (15 ml/21 g) honey

1 teaspoon (5 ml/5 g) prepared Dijon-style mustard

¼ teaspoon (1 ml) fennel seeds

1 tablespoon (15 ml) lemon juice

1 cup (250 ml/135 g) crumbled blue cheese

Salt and black pepper to taste

1. In a small bowl, stir together the mayonnaise, honey, mustard, fennel seeds, and lemon juice until it's smooth.

2. Stir in the blue cheese and season with salt and pepper.

3. Spoon the sauce over the warm, seared steaks and serve immediately.

...with Shallot and White Wine Sauce

Makes 4 Servings

This sauce also goes well on white fish, pork, and trout.

4 cooked chuck or round steaks, seared and warm
(see recipe on page 46)

1 tablespoon (15 ml/14 g) unsalted butter

1 medium shallot, peeled and finely chopped

½ cup (125 ml) dry white wine or dry vermouth

4 tablespoons (60 ml/57 g) unsalted butter, softened

2 tablespoons (30 ml/8 g) chopped fresh parsley

Salt and black pepper to taste

1. After pan-searing the steaks, put them on a warm platter and tent them with aluminum foil.

2. Pour the excess oil used to sear the steaks out of the skillet and reduce the heat to medium-low.

3. Add 1 tablespoon (1.5 ml) of the butter and the shallot to the skillet. Cook, stirring frequently, until the shallot is tender and translucent.

4. Add the wine, increase the heat to medium-high, bring to a boil, and reduce to a syrup consistency.

5. Remove the pan from the heat and whisk in the remaining butter.

6. Stir in the parsley and season with salt and pepper.

7. Pour the sauce over the warm steaks and serve immediately.

Tenderloin Roast

Makes 6–8 Servings

3–4 pounds (1.5–2 kg) beef tenderloin, trimmed

2–3 tablespoons (30–40 ml) vegetable oil (optional)

Salt and black pepper

1. Preheat the water bath to 125°F (50°C) for rare, 130°F (55°C) for medium-rare, or 140°F (60°C) for medium.

2. If the tenderloin is too long to fit into the water bath, divide it into pieces.

3. Vacuum-seal each piece of tenderloin in a separate pouch.

4. Put the sealed pouch(es) into the preheated water bath and cook for 1½–2 hours.

Pasteurization: When serving immune compromised individuals, cook the thawed tenderloin for either 3 hours at 130°F (55°C) or 2 hours at 140°F (60°C) to ensure that it's safe for them to eat. Pasteurization may give the tenderloin a mushy or pappy texture because it's already so tender.

5. Preheat a gas or charcoal grill until it's very hot.

6. Remove the tenderloin from the pouch(es) and pat the surface dry with paper towels.

7. Rub the tenderloin with the oil and generously season it with salt and pepper.

8. Sear each side of the tenderloin on the very hot grill until it's mahogany brown in color.

> *Alternative: The tenderloin can also be seared in a smoking-hot skillet.*
> *1. Pour just enough high-smoke-point oil into a heavy skillet to cover the bottom. Heat the oil over high heat, watching carefully, until it just begins to smoke.*
> *2. Working in batches, if necessary, to avoid overcrowding the skillet, sear each side of the roast until it's a deep mahogany brown, about 20–30 seconds per side.*
> *3. After searing, blot the roast with a paper towel to remove excess oil.*

9. Slice the tenderloin and serve immediately.

Top Loin (Strip), Rib-Eye, or Prime Rib Roast

Makes 6–10 Servings

3–5 pound (1.5–2.5 kg) top loin (strip), rib-eye, or prime rib roast
2–3 tablespoons (30–40 ml) vegetable oil (optional)
Salt and black pepper

1. Preheat the water bath to 125°F (50°C) for a rare roast, 130°F (55°C) for a medium-rare roast, or 140°F (60°C) for a medium roast.

2. Preheat a gas or charcoal grill until it's very hot.

3. Sear all sides of the roast until it's lightly browned.

> *Alternative: The roast can also be seared in a smoking-hot skillet.*
> *1. Pour just enough high-smoke-point oil into a heavy skillet to cover the bottom. Heat the oil over high heat, watching carefully, until it just begins to smoke.*
> *2. Sear each side of the roast until it's lightly brown, about 15–20 seconds per side.*
> *3. After searing, blot the roast with a paper towel to remove excess oil.*

4. Vacuum-seal the roast in a large pouch.

5. Put the sealed pouch into the water bath and cook a top loin (strip) roast for 2–3 hours, a rib roast for 3–4 hours at 125°F (50°C) or for 8–12 hours at either 130°F (55°C) or 140°F (60°C) (see note on page 34).

Pasteurization: When serving immune compromised individuals, cook the thawed roast for at least 4 hours at 130°F (55°C) or 3 hours at 140°F (60°C) to ensure that it's safe for them to eat.

6. Just before serving, preheat the grill again until it's very hot.

7. Remove the roast from its pouch and pat it dry with paper towels.

8. Rub the meat with oil and generously season it with salt and pepper.

9. Sear each side of the roast until it's mahogany brown in color.

> *Alternative: The roast can also be seared in a smoking-hot skillet.*
> *1. Pour just enough high-smoke-point oil into a heavy skillet to cover the bottom. Heat the oil over high heat, watching carefully, until it just begins to smoke.*
> *2. Sear each side of the roast until it's a deep mahogany brown, about 30–45 seconds per side.*
> *3. After searing, blot the roast with a paper towel to remove excess oil.*

10. Slice the roast and serve immediately.

Roast Beef

...with Garlic and Parsley Sauce
Makes 8–10 Servings

This sauce is also great on chicken, white fish, lamb, pork, rabbit, salmon, and shellfish. For some variety, consider adding a few chopped fresh mint leaves or some sautéed mushrooms.

3–5 pound (1.5–2.5 kg) cooked roast, seared, sliced, and warm (see recipe on pages 50 or 51)

3 large egg yolks, pasteurized as on page 164

Juice of 1 lemon, about 3 tablespoons (45 ml)

2 cloves (6 g) peeled garlic, minced or pressed

¼ teaspoon (1 ml) dry mustard

¼ teaspoon (1 ml) paprika

16 tablespoons (240 ml/225 g) unsalted butter, cut into pieces

1 tablespoon (15 ml/4 g) chopped fresh parsley

1 tablespoon (15 ml/3 g) chopped fresh chives

Salt and pepper to taste

1. In a saucepan, whisk together the egg yolks, lemon juice, garlic, mustard, and paprika until smooth.

2. Add the butter and put the pan over medium-low heat. Cook, whisking slowly, until all the butter melts.

3. Continue to cook, whisking constantly, until the sauce just thickens (around 160°F/70°C).

4. Remove the sauce from the heat, stir in the parsley and chives, and season with salt and pepper.

> *Alternative: You can also make this sauce sous vide.*
> *1. Preheat a water bath to 148°F (64.5°C).*
> *2. Combine the egg yolks, lemon juice, garlic, mustard, paprika, and butter into a heat-stable, resealable pouch. Squeeze all the air out of the pouch and seal.*
> *3. Put the sealed pouch into the preheated water bath. Remove the pouch, agitate the contents, and return it to the water bath every few minutes until the butter has completely melted. Then remove, agitate the contents, and replace the pouch every 5–10 minutes until the sauce has thickened, about 20–30 minutes of total cooking time.*
> *4. Just before serving, remove the pouch from the water bath, stir in the parsley and chives, and season with salt and pepper.*

5. Slice the warm roast, top it with the sauce, and serve immediately.

Chuck, Sirloin, or Round Roast
Makes 8–10 Servings

This is my favorite sous vide recipe. It transforms chuck roast, one of the least expensive cuts of beef, into something as tender and flavorful as prime rib!

4–5 pound (2–2.5 kg) chuck, tri-tip or round roast, trimmed of excess fat
2–3 tablespoons (30–40 ml) vegetable oil (optional)
Salt and black pepper

1. Preheat the water bath to 130°F (55°C) for medium-rare or 140°F (60°C) for medium (for well done, see the recipe on page 57).

2. Preheat a gas or charcoal grill until it's very hot.

3. Sear each side of the roast on the hot grill until it's lightly browned, about 1–2 minutes per side.

> *Alternative: The roast can also be seared in a smoking-hot skillet.*
> *1. Pour just enough high-smoke-point oil into a heavy skillet to cover the bottom. Heat the oil over high heat, watching carefully, until it just begins to smoke.*
> *2. Sear each side of the roast until it's lightly brown, about 20–40 seconds per side.*
> *3. After searing, blot the roast with a paper towel to remove excess oil.*

4. Vacuum-seal the roast in a large pouch.

5. Put the sealed pouch into the water bath and cook a chuck roast for 1–2 days (24–48 hours), a tri-tip roast for 8–12 hours, or a round roast for 2–3 days (48–72 hours).

6. Before serving, again preheat a grill until it's very hot.

7. Remove the roast from the pouch and pat it dry with paper towels. It's normal for the meat to have a slight greenish-brown color and for the liquid in the pouch to be reddish.

8. Rub the roast with oil and generously season it with salt and pepper.

9. Sear each side of the roast on the very hot grill until it's mahogany brown in color.

> *Alternative: The roast can also be seared in a smoking-hot skillet.*
> *1. Pour just enough high-smoke-point oil into a heavy skillet to cover the bottom. Heat the oil over high heat, watching carefully, until it just begins to smoke.*
> *2. Sear each side of the roast until it's a deep mahogany brown, about 30–45 seconds per side.*
> *3. After searing, blot the roast with a paper towel to remove excess oil.*

10. Slice the roast and serve immediately.

Roast Beef

...with Zucchini and Mint Sauce

Makes 4–6 Servings

This sauce also goes well with white fish, lamb, salmon, and shellfish.

4–5 pound (2–2.5 kg) cooked roast, seared, sliced, and warm
(see recipe on page 53)

2 tablespoons (30 ml) olive oil

1 medium onion, peeled and finely chopped, about ¾ cup (110 g)

1 medium zucchini, diced, about 1½ cups (200 g)

1 can (14½ ounce/412 g) diced tomatoes, drained

½ teaspoon (2 ml) dried thyme

½ teaspoon (2 ml) dried rosemary

Juice of 1 lemon, about 3 tablespoons (45 ml)

¼ cup (60 ml/23 g) chopped fresh spearmint leaves

Salt and black pepper to taste

1. Heat the oil in a large saucepan over medium heat.

2. Add the onion and cook, stirring occasionally, until it's tender and translucent.

3. Add the zucchini and continue to cook, stirring occasionally, until it's tender.

4. Stir in the tomatoes, thyme, rosemary, and lemon juice. Continue cooking, stirring frequently, until heated through.

5. Stir in the mint.

6. Reduce the heat to low and season with salt and pepper.

7. Spoon the sauce over the slices of cooked roast and serve immediately.

Roast Beef
...with Carrot and Leek Sauce
Makes 6–8 Servings

This sauce also goes well with chicken, duck, white fish, lamb, rabbit, salmon, shellfish, and turkey.

4–5 pound (2–2.5 kg) cooked roast, seared, sliced, and warm
(see recipe on page 53)

4 tablespoons (60 ml/57 g) unsalted butter

3 cups (750 ml/400 g) thinly sliced carrots

1 cup (250 ml/100 g) chopped leeks, white and light green part only

2 cloves (6 g) peeled garlic, minced or pressed

1 teaspoon (5 ml) tomato paste

½ teaspoon (2 ml) dried thyme

3 tablespoons (45 ml/24 g) flour

2 cups (500 ml) beef stock

¼ teaspoon (1 ml) ground coriander

Juice of 1 lemon, about 3 tablespoons (45 ml)

Salt and black pepper to taste

1. Melt the butter in a large skillet over medium heat.
2. Add the carrots and leeks, and cook, stirring frequently, until they're tender.
3. Add the garlic, tomato paste, and thyme. Continue to cook until the garlic is golden brown and fragrant.
4. Stir in the flour and continue cooking until the flour smells toasty and turns a light brown.
5. Stir in the stock, coriander, and lemon juice. Continue to cook, stirring frequently, until the sauce has thickened.
6. Reduce the heat to low and season with salt and pepper.
7. Spoon the sauce over the warm roast and serve immediately.

Beef Cheek
Makes 4 Servings

2 pounds (1 kg) beef cheek, trimmed of excess fat
2–3 tablespoons (30–40 ml) vegetable oil (optional)
Salt and black pepper

1. Preheat the water bath to 130°F (55°C) for medium-rare or 140°F (60°C) for medium.

2. Vacuum-seal the cheek in a large pouch.

3. Put the sealed pouch into the water bath and cook for 2–3 days (48–72 hours).

4. When ready to serve, preheat a gas or charcoal grill until it's very hot.

5. Remove the cheek from the pouch and pat it dry with paper towels. It's normal for the meat to have a slightly greenish-brown color and for the liquid in the pouch to be reddish.

6. Rub the surface of the beef with oil and generously season it with salt and pepper.

7. Sear both sides of the cheek on the hot grill until it's mahogany brown in color.

> *Alternative: The surface can also be browned with a kitchen blowtorch. Hold the blowtorch 4–6 inches (10–15 cm) from the meat and move the flame slowly over the surface until it's mahogany brown in color.*

8. Slice the cheek and serve immediately.

Barbecued Beef

Makes 6–8 Servings

4–5 pounds (2–2.5 kg) chuck or round roast, trimmed of excess fat

2 quarts (2 l) cold water

⅓ cup (100 g) table salt (or ½ cup Morton's kosher salt
or ⅔ cup Diamond Crystal kosher salt)

⅓ cup (50 g) smoked salt

½ cup (125 ml) barbecue sauce, store-bought
or from the recipe on page 88 or 89

1. In a large container, make a brine by adding the salts to the cold water and stirring until they're completely dissolved.

2. Cut the roast into 1½–2 inch (4–5 cm) thick slices.

3. Put the beef into the brine, cover, and refrigerate it for 12–24 hours.

4. Preheat the water bath to either 160°F (70°C) or 175°F (80°C).

5. Rinse the beef under cold running water to remove excess salt from the brine.

6. Vacuum-seal each piece of beef in a separate pouch.

7. Put the sealed pouches into the water bath and cook for 1 day (24 hours) at 160°F (70°C) or for 10–14 hours at 175°F (80°C).

8. Remove the pouches from the water bath and let them cool on the counter for about 15 minutes.

> Freezing: You can freeze the cooked beef for up to a year.
> 1. Put the sealed pouches into an ice water bath that's at least half ice for about two hours.
> 2. Dry off the pouches with a towel and put them into a freezer.
> 3. To reheat the beef, put the frozen pouches into a preheated 140°F (60°C) water bath for about an hour.

9. Remove the beef from the pouches and shred or chop it into bite-size pieces.

10. Serve on a toasted bun, if desired, with the barbecue sauce.

Beef Goulash

Makes 6–8 Servings

3–4 pounds (1.5–2 kg) chuck or round, cut into 2 inch (5 cm) cubes

High-smoke-point oil, such as grapeseed, peanut, or vegetable

2 tablespoons (30 ml/28 g) unsalted butter

4 large onions, peeled and finely chopped, about 3¾ cups (0.6 kg)

3 tablespoons (45 ml/21 g) sweet Hungarian paprika

1 jar (12 ounces/340 g) roasted red bell pepper, drained and well rinsed

1 tablespoon (15 ml) tomato paste

¼ cup (60 ml) white wine vinegar

2 tablespoons (30 ml/28 g) unsalted butter

2 tablespoons (45 ml/16 g) flour

2 cups (500 ml) beef stock

¼ cup (60 ml/58 g) sour cream

Salt and black pepper to taste

1. Preheat the water bath to 175°F (80°C).

2. Pour just enough oil into a heavy skillet to cover the bottom. Heat the oil over high heat, watching carefully, until it just begins to smoke.

3. Sear the beef cubes in batches until they're a deep brown in color on all sides, about 15–30 seconds per side.

4. Divide the beef cubes among four large, heat-stable, resealable pouches, but don't seal.

5. Melt the butter in a skillet over medium heat.

6. Add the onions and cook, stirring occasionally, until tender and translucent.

7. Divide the cooked onions among the pouches with the beef.

8. In a blender, process the paprika, roasted bell peppers, tomato paste, and vinegar until the mixture is smooth.

9. Divide the paprika mixture among the pouches.

10. Squeeze all the air out of the pouches and seal.

11. Put the sealed pouches into the water bath and cook for 10–14 hours.

12. Just before serving, melt the butter in a large saucepan over medium heat.

13. Stir in the flour and cook until it smells toasty and turns a light brown.

14. Add the stock and continue to cook, stirring occasionally, until the sauce has thickened.

15. Remove the pouches from the water bath and carefully pour their contents into the saucepan.

16. Stir in the sour cream and continue cooking until it's heated through, about 5–10 minutes.

17. Season with salt and pepper and serve immediately.

Variation: Substitute an equal amount of pork shoulder for the beef.

Braised Short Ribs

Makes 4 Servings

8–12 short ribs, about 3–4 pounds (1.5–2 kg)

High-smoke-point oil, such as grapeseed, peanut, or vegetable

¼ cup (60 ml) barbecue sauce, store-bought
or from the recipe on page 88 or 89

1. Preheat the water bath to 130°F (55°C) for medium-rare, to 140°F (60°C) for medium, or 175°F (80°C) for well done.

2. Pour just enough oil into a heavy skillet to cover the bottom. Heat the oil over high heat, watching carefully, until it just begins to smoke.

3. Sear the top and sides of the short ribs until they're a deep mahogany brown, about 15–25 seconds per side. If necessary, work in batches to avoid overcrowding the skillet.

4. Vacuum-seal the short ribs in one or more pouches so that they're in a single layer.

5. Put the sealed pouch(es) into the water bath and cook for 10–14 hours at 175°F (80°C) or for 1–2 days (24–48 hours) at either 130°F (55°C) or 140°F (60°C).

6. Remove the pouches from the water bath and let them cool on the counter for about 15 minutes.

> *Freezing: You can freeze the cooked short ribs for up to a year.*
> *1. Put the sealed pouches into an ice water bath that's at least half ice for about 45 minutes.*
> *2. Dry the pouches off with a towel and put them into a freezer.*
> *3. To reheat the ribs, put the frozen pouches into a preheated 130°F (55°C) water bath for about 45 minutes.*

7. Remove the ribs from the pouches, pat them dry with paper towels, and immediately serve them with the barbecue sauce.

Braised Short Ribs
...with Orange Barbecue Sauce
Makes 4 Servings

This sauce is also great on chicken, beef, lamb, and pork.

8–12 braised short ribs, warm (see recipe on page 60)

2 tablespoons (30 ml/28 g) unsalted butter

1 small onion, peeled and finely chopped, about ½ cup (70 g)

1 teaspoon (5 ml/3 g) ground cinnamon

½ teaspoon (2 ml) ground coriander

¼ teaspoon (1 ml) ground ginger

¼ teaspoon (1 ml) cayenne pepper

1 tablespoon (15 ml/15 g) tomato paste

1 cup (250 ml) orange juice

1 tablespoon (15 ml/8 g) cornstarch

1 tablespoon (15 ml) molasses

Salt and black pepper to taste

1. Melt the butter in a skillet over medium heat.

2. Add the onion and cook, stirring frequently, until it's tender and translucent.

3. Add the cinnamon, coriander, ginger, and cayenne and continue cooking until the spices are fragrant.

4. Stir in the tomato paste.

5. In a small bowl, stir the cornstarch into the orange juice to make a slurry.

6. Add the orange juice slurry and the molasses to the skillet. Continue to cook, stirring continually, until the sauce has cleared and thickened.

7. Reduce the heat to low and season with salt and pepper.

8. When ready to serve, remove the ribs from their pouches and top them with the sauce. Serve immediately.

Braised Oxtail

Makes 4 Servings

This recipe goes especially well with mashed potatoes or over cheese-filled tortellini and topped with grated pecorino cheese.

3–4 pounds (1.5–2 kg) oxtail separated at the joints

2 tablespoons (30 ml) olive oil

1 large onion, peeled and finely chopped, about 1 cup (150 g)

¼ teaspoon (1 ml) baking soda

½ cup (125 ml) dry red wine

1 bay leaf

½ teaspoon (2 ml) dried thyme

1 can (14½ ounce/412 g) diced tomatoes, drained

Salt and black pepper to taste

1. Preheat the water bath to 175°F (80°C).

2. Heat the oil in a skillet over medium heat.

3. Add the onion and cook until it's tender and translucent.

4. Sprinkle baking soda over the onion and continue cooking, stirring frequently, until it's golden brown.

5. Add the wine and continue to cook until it's been reduced by at least half.

6. Stir in the bay leaf, thyme, and tomatoes.

7. Remove the tomato mixture from the heat and set it aside.

8. Put the oxtail and tomato mixture into one or more large, resealable pouches. Squeeze all the air out of the pouch and seal.

9. Put the sealed pouch(es) into the water bath and cook for 12–18 hours.

10. Remove the cooked oxtail from the pouch(es), put the meat onto a warm platter, and tent it with aluminum foil to keep it warm.

11. Pour the liquid from the pouch into a saucepan and remove the bay leaf.

12. Bring the liquid to a simmer over medium heat and cook until it's reduced in volume and thickened.

13. Season with salt and pepper.

14. Pour the sauce over the oxtail and serve immediately.

Beef Brisket
Makes 6–8 Servings

3–4 pounds (1.5–2 kg) beef brisket, slits cut in the fat cap in a crosshatch pattern

½ cup (125 ml) barbecue sauce, store-bought or from the recipe on page 88 or 89

1. Preheat the water bath to 130°F (55°C) for medium-rare, 140°F (60°C) for medium, or 175°F (80°C) for well done.

2. Preheat a gas or charcoal grill until it's very hot.

3. Pat the brisket dry with paper towels.

4. Sear the brisket on the hot grill until the fat is golden brown and the meat is lightly browned.

5. Divide the brisket into pieces so that it will fit into the vacuum pouches, and vacuum-seal each piece in a separate pouch.

6. Put the sealed pouches into the water bath and cook for 12–24 hours at 175°F (80°C) or for 2–3 days (48–72 hours) at either 130°F (55°C) or 140°F (60°C).

> *Freezing: The cooked brisket can be frozen for up to a year.*
> *1. Put the still sealed pouches into an ice water bath that's at least half ice for about an hour.*
> *2. Dry the pouches off with a towel and put them into a freezer.*
> *3. To reheat the beef, put the frozen pouches into a preheated 130°F (55°C) water bath for about 45 minutes.*

7. Slice the brisket across the grain into long, thin slices and serve with the barbecue sauce.

Corned Beef Brisket

Makes 6 Servings

You can cure your own beef brisket in about a week.

4–5 pounds (2–2½ kg) beef brisket, fat trimmed off

2 quarts (2 l) cold water

8 ounces (225 g) kosher salt, about ¾ cup table salt, 1 cups Morton's kosher, or 1½ cups Diamond Crystal kosher salt

¼ cup (60 ml/55 g) brown sugar

1 tablespoon (15 ml/8 g) pickling spice

1 tablespoon (15 ml/15 g) pink (curing) salt

1. Make a brine by stirring the salt, sugar, pickling spice, and pink (curing) salt into the cold water until the salts and sugar have dissolved completely.

2. Put the trimmed brisket into the brine and cover tightly.

3. Refrigerate the brisket in the brine for 5–10 days. Flip the brisket in the brine once each day.

4. Rinse the brisket thoroughly under cold running water to remove excess salt and sugar.

5. Preheat the water bath to 160°F (70°C).

6. Divide the corned brisket into pieces so that it will fit into the vacuum pouches, and vacuum-seal each piece in a separate pouch.

7. Put the sealed pouches into the water bath and cook for 1–2 days (24–48 hours).

...with Cabbage Relish

2 tablespoons (30 ml) olive oil

½ medium head green cabbage, sliced, about 5 cups (450 g)

1 large onion, peeled and sliced, about 1 cup (150 g)

1 teaspoon (5 ml/3 g) mustard seeds

¼ teaspoon (2 ml) dried thyme

1 tablespoon (15 ml) white vinegar

Salt and black pepper to taste

8. Before serving, heat the oil in a saucepan over medium heat.

9. Add the cabbage and onion. Cook, stirring frequently, until the onion and cabbage are tender and translucent.

10. Add the mustard seeds and thyme, and continue cooking until it's fragrant.

11. Reduce the heat to low and add the vinegar.

12. Season with salt and pepper.

13. Remove the brisket from the pouch, pat dry with paper towels, slice across the grain into long, thin slices, and serve immediately on a bed of the cabbage relish.

Slow Cooked Pork Chops

Makes 4 Servings

4 (1½ inches/4 cm thick) loin, rib, or sirloin pork chops
Salt and black pepper
High-smoke-point oil, such as grapeseed, peanut, or vegetable

1. Preheat the water bath to 130°F (55°C).
2. Vacuum-seal each chop in a separate pouch.
3. Put the sealed pouches into the water bath and cook loin chops for at least 2½ hours, rib chops for 6–8 hours, or sirloin chops for 8–12 hours.

Freezing: The cooked chops can be frozen for up to a year.
1. To freeze, put the sealed pouches into an ice water bath that's at least half ice for about an hour.
2. Dry off the pouches with a towel and put them into a freezer.
3. To reheat the chops, put the frozen pouches into a preheated 130°F (55°C) water bath for about 45 minutes.

4. Remove the chops from their pouches and pat them dry with paper towels.
5. Generously season the chops with salt and pepper.
6. Pour just enough oil into a heavy skillet to cover the bottom. Heat the oil over high heat, watching carefully, until it just begins to smoke.
7. Sear each side of the chops until it's golden brown, about 15–25 seconds per side. Work in batches, if necessary, to avoid overcrowding the skillet.
8. Remove the chops from the pan and blot them with paper towels to remove excess oil.

Alternative: The chops can also be seared on a hot grill.
1. About 15 minutes before serving, preheat a gas or charcoal grill until it's very hot.
2. Remove the chops from the pouches and pat them dry with paper towels.
3. Lightly brush the chops with oil and then generously season them with salt and pepper.
4. Put the chops on the very hot grill and sear each side until it's golden browned, about one minute per side.

9. Serve the chops immediately.

Slow Cooked Pork Chops

...with Sweet Bacon Vinaigrette

Makes 4 Servings

This vinaigrette is also great on beef, chicken, duck, white fish, lamb, rabbit, salmon, shellfish, and venison; any leftover meat and vinaigrette is especially good on top of a spinach salad with tomatoes and mushrooms.

4 slow cooked chops, seared and warm (see recipe on page 66)

5 slices (40 g) bacon, chopped

Vegetable oil

¼ cup (60 ml) balsamic vinegar

2 tablespoons (30 ml/28 g) brown sugar

1 clove (3 g) peeled garlic, minced or pressed

1 teaspoon (5 ml/5 g) mayonnaise

½ teaspoon (2 ml) dried rosemary

Salt and black pepper to taste

1. Cook the bacon in a skillet over medium heat until crispy.

2. Remove the bacon with a slotted spoon, crumble and set aside until needed.

3. Pour the bacon fat into a measuring cup and add enough vegetable oil to make ¾ cup (175 ml).

4 Put the vinegar, brown sugar, garlic, mayonnaise, and rosemary into a blender and process until smooth.

5. With the motor running, add the bacon fat mixture in a thin, steady stream.

6. Transfer the vinaigrette to a bowl and stir in the reserved bacon.

7. Season with salt and pepper.

8. Pour the sauce over the warm, seared chops and serve immediately.

...with Apple and Orange Sauce

Makes 4 Servings

4 slow cooked chops, seared and warm (see recipe on page 66)

2 tablespoons (30 ml/28 g) unsalted butter

2 medium apples, peeled and diced, about 3 cups (320 g)

1 tablespoon (15 ml/14 g) brown sugar

1 cup (250 ml) orange juice

1 tablespoon (15 ml/8 g) cornstarch

1 teaspoon (5 ml/2 g) ground ginger

Salt to taste

1. Melt the butter in a skillet over medium heat.

2. Add the apples and brown sugar and cook, stirring frequently, until tender and lightly browned.

3. In a small bowl, stir the cornstarch into the orange juice to make a slurry.

4. Add the orange juice slurry and ginger to the skillet. Continue to cook, stirring frequently, until thickened.

5. Reduce the heat to low and season with salt.

6. Spoon the sauce over the warm chops and serve immediately.

Slow Cooked Pork Chops

Slow Cooked Pork Chops

...with Spicy Soy Sauce

Makes 4 Servings

This sauce is great with or without the optional mushrooms; it's also great on beef, chicken, duck, white fish, shellfish, and venison.

4 slow cooked chops, seared and warm (see recipe on page 66)

1 tablespoon (15 ml) olive oil

8 ounces (225 g) fresh mushrooms, thinly sliced (optional)

2 cloves (60 g) peeled garlic, minced or pressed

1 tablespoon (15 ml/6 g) grated fresh ginger

¼ cup (60 ml) soy sauce

¼ cup (60 ml) mirin, a sweetened Japanese rice wine

½ tablespoon (7.5 ml/4 g) cornstarch

2 tablespoons (30 ml/42 g) honey

½ teaspoon (2 ml) red pepper flakes

1. Heat the olive oil in a saucepan over medium-high heat.

2. (Optional) Add the mushrooms and cook them until they're tender and lightly browned.

3. Reduce the heat to medium and add the garlic and ginger. Cook the garlic until it's golden brown and fragrant.

4. In a small bowl, stir the cornstarch into the soy sauce to make a slurry.

5. Add the slurry to the saucepan and stir in the mirin, honey, and red pepper flakes. Continue to cook, stirring constantly, until the sauce has cleared and thickened.

6. Reduce the heat to low and cover until needed.

7. Pour the sauce over the warm chops and serve immediately.

Slow Cooked Pork Chops

...with Apples and Vanilla

Makes 4 Servings

Making your own vanilla extract is easy and tastes incredible. Take 4 ounces (100 g) vanilla beans (I get mine off the internet) and split them in half lengthwise; then put them into a 1 quart (1 l) canning jar and fill the jar with a good mid-priced vodka; store in a dark place and agitate once a day for the first week or two. The extract will be usable after about two weeks and will continue to improve in depth and flavor over the next few months.

This sauce also goes well on chicken, lamb, and shellfish.

4 slow cooked chops, seared and warm (see recipe on page 66)

2 tablespoons (30 ml/28 g) unsalted butter

2 large apples, peeled and diced, about 2 ¾ cups (430 g)

1 tablespoon (15 ml/21 g) honey

Juice of 1 lemon, about 3 tablespoons (45 ml)

2 teaspoons (10 ml) vanilla extract

Salt to taste

1. Melt the butter in a skillet over medium-low heat.

2. Add the apples and cook, stirring occasionally, until they soften.

3. Increase the heat to medium and add the honey. Continue to cook, stirring frequently, until the apples are golden brown.

4. Stir in the lemon juice and the vanilla extract.

5. Reduce the heat to low and season with a pinch of salt.

6. Spoon the sauce over the warm, seared chops and serve immediately.

Slow Cooked Pork Chops

...with Cream Cheese and Apricot Sauce

Makes 4 Servings

This sauce also goes well on chicken.

4 slow cooked chops, seared and warm (see recipe on page 66)

4 ounces (120 g) cream cheese

½ cup (125 ml) heavy cream

¼ cup (60 ml/80 g) apricot preserve

Juice of 1 lemon, about 3 tablespoons (45 ml)

1 teaspoon (5 ml/5 g) prepared horseradish

Garlic salt and pepper to taste

1. In a saucepan, combine the cream cheese, heavy cream, apricot preserve, lemon juice, and horseradish.

2. Cook the mixture over medium heat, stirring frequently, until it's heated through and smooth.

3. Reduce the heat to low and season with garlic salt and pepper.

4. Spoon the sauce over the warm chops and serve immediately.

Brined Pork Chops
Makes 4 Servings

4 (1½ inches/4 cm thick) loin, rib, or sirloin pork chops

1 quart (1 l) cold water

4 tablespoons (75 g) table salt (6 tablespoons Morton's kosher salt
or ½ cup Diamond Crystal kosher salt)

2 tablespoons (25 g) granulated or brown sugar

2–3 tablespoons (30–40 ml) vegetable oil (optional)

Salt and black pepper

1. To make the brine, first put the water into a large container (or a gallon-size, resealable, plastic bag). Add the salt and sugar, and stir until they dissolve completely.

2. Add the pork chops, cover (or seal), and refrigerate for at least 2 hours.

3. Preheat the water bath to 140°F (60°C) for medium or 130°F (55°C) for medium-rare.

4. Remove the chops from the brine, and rinse them under cold, running water to remove excess salt and sugar.

5. Vacuum-seal each chop in a separate pouch.

6. Put the sealed pouches into the preheated water bath and cook for 1½–2½ hours at 140°F (60°C) or for 2½–3½ hours at 130°F (55°C).

> *Freezing: The cooked chops can be frozen for up to a year.*
> *1. Put the sealed pouches into an ice water bath that's at least half ice for about an hour.*
> *2. Dry off the pouches with a towel and put them into a freezer.*
> *3. To reheat the chops, put the frozen pouches into a preheated 130°F (55°C) water bath for about 45 minutes.*

7. Preheat a gas or charcoal grill until it's very hot.

8. Remove the chops from their pouches and pat them dry with paper towels.

9. Lightly brush the chops with oil, and generously season them with salt and pepper.

10. Put the chops on the hot grill and sear each side until it's golden brown.

> *Alternative: You can also sear the chops in a smoking-hot skillet.*
> *1. Remove the cooked chops from their pouches and pat them dry with paper towels.*
> *2. Generously season the chops with salt and pepper.*
> *3. Pour just enough high-smoke-point oil into a heavy skillet to cover the*

bottom. Heat the oil over high heat, watching carefully, until it just begins to smoke.
4. Sear each side of the chops until it's golden brown, about 15–20 seconds per side. Work in batches, if necessary, to avoid over-crowding the skillet.
5. Remove the chops from the pan and blot them with a paper towel to remove excess oil.

11. Serve the seared chops immediately.

Brined Pork Chops

...with Onion and Goat Cheese Sauce

Makes 4 Servings

This sauce also goes well on chicken, duck, lamb, shrimp, and venison.

4 cooked brined chops, seared and warm (see recipe on page 72)

2 tablespoons (30 ml/28 g) unsalted butter

1 large onion, peeled and finely chopped, about 1 cup (150 g)

1 clove (3 g) peeled garlic, minced or pressed

1 cup (250 ml/135 g) crumbled goat cheese

Juice of 1 lemon, about 3 tablespoons (45 ml)

2 tablespoons (30 ml/42 g) honey

½ teaspoon (2 ml) dried rubbed sage

½ teaspoon (2 ml) dried rosemary

Salt and black pepper to taste

1. Melt the butter in a skillet over medium heat.

2. Add the onion and cook, stirring frequently, until it's tender and translucent.

3. Add the garlic and continue cooking until it's golden brown and fragrant.

4. Add the goat cheese, lemon juice, honey, sage, and rosemary. Continue to cook, stirring constantly, until the sauce is smooth and heated through.

5. Reduce the heat to low and season with salt and pepper.

6. Spoon the sauce over the warm, seared chops and serve immediately.

Brined Pork Chops
...with Bell Pepper and Onion Relish
Makes 4 Servings

This sauce is also great on lamb and shrimp.

4 cooked brined chops, seared and warm (see recipe on page 72)

2 tablespoons (30 ml) vegetable oil

1 medium red onion, peeled and finely chopped, about ¾ cup (110 g)

2 red or yellow bell peppers, finely chopped, about 1⅔ cups (240 g)

1 tablespoon (15 ml) extra virgin olive oil

2 tablespoons (30 ml) white wine vinegar

1 teaspoon (5 ml) Worcestershire sauce

½ teaspoon (2 ml) red pepper flakes

2 tablespoons (30 ml/8 g) chopped fresh parsley

1. Heat the oil in a skillet over medium heat.

2. Add the onion and the bell peppers, and cook, stirring frequently, until both are tender and the onion is translucent.

3. Transfer the onion mixture to a bowl and stir in the olive oil, vinegar, Worcestershire sauce, red pepper flakes, and parsley.

4. Spoon the relish over the warm, seared chops and serve immediately.

Brined Pork Chops

...with Tomato and Chickpea Relish

Makes 4 Servings

This relish also goes well on chicken and lamb.

4 cooked brined chops, seared and warm (see recipe on page 72)

1 tablespoon (15 ml) olive oil

1 medium onion, peeled and finely chopped, about ¾ cup (110 g)

1 can (15 oz/425 g) chickpeas (garbanzo beans), drained and rinsed

1 can (14 ½ ounce/412 g) diced tomatoes, drained

¼ cup (60 ml/15 g) chopped fresh parsley

Garlic salt and pepper to taste

1. Heat the olive oil in a skillet over medium heat.

2. Add the onion and cook, stirring occasionally, until it's tender and translucent.

3. Add the chickpeas and tomatoes and simmer for 10 minutes to allow the flavors to meld.

4. Reduce the heat to low and stir in the parsley.

5. Season with garlic salt and pepper.

6. Spoon the sauce over the warm, seared chops and serve immediately.

...with Spinach, Mushroom, and Mustard Sauce

Makes 4 Servings

This sauce also goes well on beef, chicken, white fish, lamb, rabbit, salmon, shellfish, and venison.

4 cooked brined chops, seared and warm (see recipe on page 72)

2 tablespoons (30 g) unsalted butter

1 small onion, peeled and finely chopped, about ½ cup (70 g)

4 ounces (100 g) fresh mushrooms, thinly sliced

4 ounces (100 g) fresh baby spinach, chopped

½ cup (125 ml) sour cream

1 tablespoon (15 ml) prepared mustard

Salt and black pepper to taste

1. Melt the butter in a large skillet over medium heat.

2. Add the onion and cook, stirring frequently, until it's softened.

3. Add the mushrooms and spinach. Continue to cook, stirring frequently, until the mushrooms are tender.

4. Reduce the heat to low, and add the sour cream and mustard.

5. Season with salt and pepper.

6. Spoon the sauce over the warm, seared chops and serve immediately.

Variation: Add a handful of chopped fresh mint leaves or a ¼ teaspoon (1 ml) fennel seeds with the spinach and mushrooms.

Brined Pork Chops

...with Apple, Cabbage, and Onion

Makes 4 Servings

This sauce also goes well with beef, chicken, duck, pork, rabbit, salmon, shrimp, and venison.

4 cooked brined chops, seared and warm (see recipe on page 72)

2 tablespoons (30 ml) vegetable oil

1 medium onion, peeled and sliced, about ¾ cup (110 g)

½ medium head green cabbage, sliced, about 5 cups (450 g)

1 apple, peeled and diced, about 1½ cup (160 g)

½ teaspoon (2 ml) dried thyme

1 pinch baking soda

1 teaspoon (5 ml) prepared mustard

Juice of ½ a lemon, about 1½ tablespoons (25 ml)

2 tablespoons (30 ml/8 g) chopped fresh parsley

Salt and black pepper to taste

1. Heat the oil in a skillet over medium-low heat.

2. Add the onion, cabbage, apple, and thyme. Cook, stirring occasionally, until the onion is tender and translucent.

3. Increase the heat to medium, add the baking soda, and continue cooking, stirring frequently, until the apple and onion are golden brown.

4. Reduce the heat to low and stir in the mustard, lemon juice, and parsley.

5. Season with salt and pepper.

6. Put the warm, seared chops on a bed of the cabbage mixture and serve immediately.

Pork Tenderloin
Makes 4 Servings

1½ pounds (0.7 kg) pork tenderloin, divided into four 6 ounce (170 g) portions
2-3 tablespoons (30–40 ml) vegetable oil (optional)
Salt and black pepper

1. Preheat the water bath to 140°F (60°C) for medium or 130°F (55°C) for medium-rare.

2. Vacuum-seal each piece of tenderloin in a separate pouch.

3. Put the sealed pouches into the preheated water bath and cook for 2-3 hours at 140°F (60°C) or for 3–4 hours at 130°F (55°C).

4. Preheat a gas or charcoal grill until it's very hot.

5. Remove the pieces of tenderloin from the pouches and pat them dry with paper towels.

6. Rub the oil on the tenderloin pieces and generously season them with salt and pepper.

7. Put the pieces of tenderloin on the hot grill and sear each side until it's golden brown, about one minute per side.

> *Alternative: The tenderloin pieces can also be seared in smoking-hot oil.*
> *1. Pour just enough high-smoke-point oil into a heavy skillet to cover the bottom. Heat the oil over high heat, watching carefully, until it just begins to smoke.*
> *2. Working in batches, if necessary, to avoid overcrowding the skillet, sear each side of the tenderloin pieces until they're golden brown, about 25–40 seconds per side.*
> *3. Remove the tenderloin pieces from the skillet and pat them with a paper towel to remove excess oil.*

8. Slice the tenderloin into ½ inch (15 mm) pieces and serve immediately.

...with Honey and Lime Vinaigrette

Makes 4 Servings

This vinaigrette is also great on chicken, duck, white fish, lamb, and shellfish.

1 cooked tenderloin, seared, sliced, and warm (see recipe on page 79)

Zest and juice of 2 limes, about ¼ cup (60 ml) of juice
and 1½ tablespoon (20 ml) of zest

2 tablespoons (30 ml/42 g) honey

1 teaspoon (5 ml/5 g) prepared Dijon-style mustard

1 teaspoon (5 ml/5 g) mayonnaise

1 teaspoon (5 ml/2 g) grated fresh ginger

1 cup (250 ml) vegetable oil

2 tablespoons (30 ml/11 g) chopped fresh spearmint leaves

Salt and black pepper to taste

1. Put the lime juice, lime zest, honey, mustard, mayonnaise, and ginger into a blender and process until smooth.

2. While the motor is running, slowly add the oil in a thin, steady stream.

3. Transfer to a bowl and stir in the mint.

4. Season with salt and pepper.

5. Pour the sauce over the warm, sliced tenderloin and serve immediately.

Pork Tenderloin

Pork Tenderloin

...with Pear and Pecan Sauce

Makes 4 Servings

This sauce is also great on chicken.

1 cooked tenderloin, seared, sliced, and warm (see recipe on page 79)

½ cup (125 ml/55 g) chopped pecans

1 cup (250 ml) apple juice

1 tablespoon (15 ml/8 g) cornstarch

2 pears, peeled and diced, about 2 cups (300 g)

1 tablespoon (15 ml/21 g) honey

1 teaspoon (5 ml/3 g) ground cinnamon

Juice of ½ a lemon, about 1½ tablespoons (25 ml)

Salt and black pepper to taste

1. In a saucepan over medium heat, toast the pecans, stirring frequently, until they're fragrant and lightly browned.

2. Meanwhile, in a small bowl, whisk the cornstarch into the apple juice to make a slurry.

3. Add the apple juice slurry, pears, honey, and cinnamon to the saucepan with the toasted pecans. Cook over medium heat, stirring frequently, until the pears have softened and the sauce has cleared and thickened.

4. Reduce the heat to low and stir in the lemon juice.

5. Season with salt and pepper.

6. Spoon the sauce over the warm, sliced tenderloin and serve immediately.

Pork Tenderloin

...with Pineapple and Mango Sauce

Makes 4 Servings

This sauce is also great with chicken, tropical fish, salmon, and shellfish.

1 cooked tenderloin, seared, sliced, and warm (see recipe on page 79)

1 cup (250 ml) pineapple juice

1 tablespoon (15 ml/8 g) cornstarch

2 tablespoons (30 ml/28 g) brown sugar or honey

2 teaspoons (10 ml/4 g) grated fresh ginger

1 ripe mango, peeled, seeded, and diced, about 1⅓ cups (200 g)

Salt and black pepper to taste

1. In a small bowl, whisk the cornstarch into the pineapple juice to make a slurry.

2. In a saucepan over medium heat, combine the slurry, brown sugar (or honey), ginger, and mango. Cook, stirring frequently, until the mango has softened and the sauce has cleared and thickened.

3. Reduce the heat to low and season with salt and pepper.

4. Pour the sauce over the warm, sliced tenderloin and serve immediately.

Pork Tenderloin

...with Apples and Pears

Makes 4 Servings

This relish is also great on duck.

1 cooked tenderloin, seared, sliced, and warm (see recipe on page 79)

2 tablespoons (30 ml/28 g) unsalted butter

2 apples, peeled and diced, about 2 ¾ cups (300 g)

1 pear, peeled and diced, about 1 cup (150 g)

1 teaspoon (5 ml) fresh rosemary

½ teaspoon (2 ml) fennel seeds

1 tablespoon (15 ml/21 g) honey

Juice of ½ a lemon, about 1 ½ tablespoons (25 ml)

Salt and black pepper to taste

1. Melt the butter in a skillet over medium heat.

2. Add the apples, pear, rosemary, and fennel seeds. Cook, stirring occasionally, until the apples and pear have softened.

3. Add the honey and continue to cook, stirring frequently, until the apples and pear are golden brown.

4. Reduce the heat to low, stir in the lemon juice, and season with salt and pepper

5. Spoon the relish over the warm, sliced tenderloin and serve immediately.

Pulled Pork
Makes 8–20 Servings

9–15 pound (4–7 kg) boneless Boston butt, trimmed of excess hard, waxy fat

1 gallon (4 l) cold water

1 cup (300 g) table salt or, preferably, 1 cup (200 g) Morton's kosher salt (1⅓ cups Diamond Crystal kosher salt) and ½ cup (100 g) smoked salt

Barbecue sauce, store-bought or from the recipe on page 88 or 89

1. In a large, food-safe container, make the brine by stirring the salt(s) into the cold water until they've completely dissolved.

2. Cut the pork into 1½–2 inch (4–5 cm) thick slices, put them into the brine, cover, and refrigerate them for ½–2 days (12–48 hours).

3. When ready to cook, preheat the water bath to either 160°F (70°C) or 175°F (80°C) as described in step 6.

4. Remove the pork from the brine and rinse it under cold, running water to remove excess salt.

5. Vacuum-seal each piece of pork in a separate pouch.

6. Put the sealed pouches into the preheated water bath and cook for 1 day (24 hours) at 160°F (70°C) or for 8–12 hours at 175°F (80°C).

7. Remove the pork from the water bath and let the pouches cool on the counter for about 15 minutes.

> *Freezing: The cooked pork can be frozen for up to a year.*
> *1. Put the still sealed pouches into an ice water bath that's at least half ice for about two hours, adding additional ice as necessary.*
> *2. Dry off the pouches with a towel and put them into a freezer.*
> *3. To reheat the pork, put the frozen pouches into a preheated 140°F (60°C) water bath for about an hour.*

8. Remove the pork from the pouches and shred or chop it into bite-size pieces.

9. Serve on a toasted bun, if desired, with the barbecue sauce.

> *Variation: For Mexican style pulled pork, fry the shredded or chopped pork in 375°F (190°C) lard (or oil) until lightly browned. Serve in a warm tortilla with some chopped red onion, salsa (such as pico de gallo), and guacamole.*

...with Black Bean Salsa

Makes 4 Servings

1½ pounds (0.7 kg) cooked pulled pork, warm and in bite-size pieces (see recipe on page 84)

2 tablespoons (30 ml) lard or vegetable oil

1 small onion, peeled and finely chopped, about ½ cup (70 g)

1 clove (3 g) peeled garlic, minced or pressed

¼ cup (60 ml/40 g) corn kernels, fresh or frozen

1 can (15 ounce/425 g) black beans, drained and rinsed

1 medium tomato, seeded and chopped, about ¾ cup (120 g)

1 small jalapeño chile, seeded and chopped, about 1 tablespoon (14 g)

¼ cup (60 ml/4 g) chopped fresh cilantro

⅓ cup (80 ml) red wine vinegar

Salt and black pepper to taste

1. In a skillet over medium heat, melt the lard (or heat the oil).

2. Add the onion and cook, stirring frequently, until it's tender and translucent.

3. Add the garlic and continue to cook until it's golden brown and fragrant.

4. Add the corn and continue cooking, stirring frequently, until it's tender and lightly browned.

5. Stir in the black beans, tomato, and jalapeño pepper, and continue to cook until it's heated through.

6. Transfer to a bowl and stir in the cilantro and vinegar.

7. Season with salt and pepper.

8. Serve the pulled pork with the salsa.

Barbecued Spareribs
Makes 4 Servings

1 (3–5 pound/1.4–2.3 kg) spare ribs, trimmed

½ cup (125 ml) barbecue sauce, store-bought or from the recipe on page 88 or 89

Dry Rub

2 tablespoons (30 ml/14 g) paprika

1½ tablespoons (20 ml/7 g) celery salt

1½ tablespoons (20 ml/13 g) garlic powder

1 tablespoon (15 ml/6 g) ground black pepper

1 tablespoon (15 ml/8 g) chili powder

1 tablespoon (15 ml/8 g) ground cumin

1 tablespoon (15 ml/14 g) brown sugar

1 tablespoon (15 ml/18 g) table salt

1 teaspoon (5 ml/4 g) granulated sugar

1 teaspoon (5 ml/2 g) dried oregano

1 teaspoon (5 ml/2 g) cayenne pepper

1. Preheat the water bath to 175°F (80°C).

2. Divide the spare ribs into four pieces.

3. Pat the ribs dry with paper towels and generously season them with the dry rub.

4. Vacuum-seal each section of ribs in a separate pouch.

5. Put the sealed pouches into the water bath and cook them for 8–12 hours.

6. Remove the ribs from the water bath and let the pouches cool on the counter for about 15 minutes.

> Freezing: The cooked ribs can be frozen for up to a year.
> 1. Put the still sealed pouches into an ice water bath that's at least half ice for about 1½ hours, adding additional ice as necessary.
> 2. Dry off the pouches with a towel and put them into a freezer.
> 3. To reheat the pork, put the frozen pouches into a preheated 140°F (60°C) water bath for about an hour.

7. Remove the ribs from their pouches and pat them dry with paper towels.

8. Brush the cooked ribs with the barbecue sauce and serve immediately.

Sweet and Sour Spareribs
Makes 4 Servings

1 (3–5 pound/1.4–2.3 kg) spare ribs, trimmed

¼ cup (60 ml) soy sauce

1 tablespoon (15 ml/8 g) cornstarch

1 can (8 ounce/226 g) pineapple chunks with liquid

¼ cup (50 g) brown sugar

2 tablespoons (30 ml) rice wine vinegar

1 tablespoon (6 g) grated fresh ginger

Salt and black pepper to taste

1. Preheat the water bath to 175°F (80°C).

2. Divide the spare ribs into four pieces.

3. Vacuum-seal each section of ribs in a separate pouch

4. Put the sealed pouches into the water bath and cook them for 8–12 hours.

5. Before serving, whisk the cornstarch into the soy sauce to make a slurry.

6. Combine the soy sauce slurry, pineapple, sugar, vinegar, and ginger in a saucepan. Cook over medium heat, stirring frequently, until the sauce has cleared and thickened.

7. Reduce the heat to low and season with salt and pepper.

8. Serve the cooked ribs topped with the sweet and sour sauce.

Spicy Vinegar Barbecue Sauce

Makes 6 Servings

This barbecue sauce is also great on chicken and beef.

½ cup (125 ml) white vinegar

½ cup (125 ml) cider vinegar

½ cup (125 ml/110 g) brown sugar

1 can (6 ounces/170 g) tomato paste

1 tablespoon (15 ml) molasses

1½ teaspoons (7.5 ml) Tabasco® sauce

1 teaspoon (5 ml/2 g) red pepper flakes

1 teaspoon (5 ml/2 g) coarse ground black pepper

1. Mix the vinegars, sugar, tomato paste, molasses, Tabasco sauce, red pepper flakes, and pepper together in a small saucepan.

2. Bring it to a simmer over medium heat, stirring frequently.

3. Reduce the heat to low and cover until needed.

4. Serve immediately or refrigerate for up to a week.

Mild Mustard Barbecue Sauce

Makes 6 Servings

This barbecue sauce is also great on beef, chicken, duck, lamb, rabbit, and venison. For a spicier version of this sauce, add 1 teaspoon (5 ml) Tabasco® sauce.

2 tablespoons (30 ml/28 g) unsalted butter

1 medium onion, peeled and finely chopped, about ¾ cup (110 g)

1 clove (3 g) peeled garlic, minced or pressed

1½ tablespoons (25 ml/10 g) chili powder

1 cup (250 ml) ketchup

½ cup (125 ml) cider vinegar

2 tablespoons (30 ml) prepared spicy brown or Dijon-style mustard

2 tablespoons (30 ml) Worcestershire sauce

½ teaspoon (2 ml) celery seeds

¼ cup (60 ml/55 g) brown sugar

1. Melt the butter in saucepan over medium heat.

2. Add the onion and cook, stirring frequently, until tender and translucent.

3. Add the garlic and chili powder, and continue to cook until they're fragrant.

4. Add the ketchup, vinegar, mustard, Worcestershire sauce, celery seeds, and brown sugar and continue cooking, stirring frequently, until the sauce comes to a simmer.

5. Reduce the heat to low and cover until needed.

6. Serve immediately or refrigerate for up to a week.

Pan-Seared Lamb Chops

Makes 4 Servings

4 (8 ounce/225 g) loin or rib chops
High-smoke-point oil, such as grapeseed, peanut, or vegetable
Salt and black pepper

1. Preheat the water bath to 125°F (50°C) for a rare chop, 130°F (55°C) for a medium-rare chop, or 140°F (60°C) for a medium chop.

2. Vacuum-seal each chop in a separate pouch. Wrap the bones, if present, with parchment paper or aluminum foil to prevent them from piercing the pouch.

3. Put the sealed pouches into the water bath and cook for 1–1½ hours.

Pasteurization: When serving immune compromised individuals, cook a 1–1¼ inch (25–30 mm) thick chop for either 2 hours at 130°F (55°C) or 1 hour at 140°F (60°C) to ensure that it's safe for them to eat.

4. Remove the chops from their pouches, pat them dry with paper towels, and generously season them with salt and pepper.

5. Pour just enough oil into a heavy skillet to cover the bottom. Heat the oil over high heat, watching carefully, until it just begins to smoke.

6. Sear each side of the chops until they're a deep mahogany brown, about 15–25 seconds per side. Work in batches, if necessary, to avoid crowding the skillet.

7. Blot the seared chops with a paper towel to remove excess oil.

Alternative: The chops can also be finished on the grill.
1. About 15 minutes before serving, preheat a gas or charcoal grill until it's very hot.
2. Remove the chops from their pouches and pat them dry with paper towels.
3. Lightly brush the chops with oil and generously season them with salt and pepper.
4. Put the chops on the very hot grill and sear each side until it's mahogany brown in color, about one minute per side.

8. Serve immediately.

Pan-Seared Lamb Chops

...with Fig and Honey Sauce

Makes 4 Servings

This sauce also goes well on chicken, duck, and pork.

4 cooked lamb chops, seared and warm (see recipe on page 90)

1 cup (250 ml) chicken stock, room temperature or cooler

1 tablespoon (15 ml/8 g) cornstarch

1 cup (250 ml/150 g) dried figs, chopped

2 tablespoons (30 ml/42 g) honey

1 tablespoon (15 ml/6 g) grated fresh ginger

Juice of ½ a lemon, about 1½ tablespoons (25 ml)

Salt and black pepper to taste

1. Whisk the cornstarch into the stock to make a slurry.

2. Combine the slurry, figs, honey, ginger, and lemon juice in a saucepan. Cook over medium heat, stirring occasionally, until the sauce has cleared and thickened.

3. Reduce the heat to low and season with salt and pepper.

4. Spoon the sauce over the warm, seared lamb chops and serve immediately.

Pan-Seared Lamb Chops

...with Mint Pesto

Makes 4 Servings

This pesto is also great on beef, chicken, duck, white fish, pork, rabbit, salmon, and shellfish.

4 cooked lamb chops, seared and warm (see recipe on page 90)

½ cup (125 ml/60 g) crushed walnuts

1½ cups (375 ml/37 g) chopped fresh spearmint leaves

½ cup (125 ml/12 g) fresh basil leaves

¼ cup (60 ml) extra virgin olive oil

2 cloves (6 g) peeled garlic, minced or pressed

Zest and juice of 1 lemon, about 3 tablespoons (45 ml) of juice and 1 tablespoon (15 ml) of zest

¾ cup (175 ml/75 g) grated Parmesan cheese

Salt and black pepper to taste

1. Put the walnuts, mint, basil, oil, garlic, lemon juice and zest, and Parmesan cheese into a blender or food processor and pulse until smooth.

2. Season with salt and pepper.

3. Spoon the pesto over the warm, seared lamb chops and serve immediately.

Pan-Seared Lamb Chops

...with Orange and Mint Vinaigrette

Makes 4 Servings

This vinaigrette is also great on duck or on a salad topped with chicken or shellfish.

4 cooked lamb chops, seared and warm (see recipe on page 90)

¼ cup (60 ml) orange juice

1 tablespoon (15 ml/21 g) honey

2 tablespoons (30 ml/11 g) chopped fresh spearmint leaves

1 tablespoon (15 ml/6 g) grated fresh ginger

2 teaspoons (10 ml/4 g) unsweetened cocoa powder

1 teaspoon (5 ml/5 g) mayonnaise

¾ cup (175 ml) vegetable oil

Salt and black pepper to taste

1. Put the orange juice, honey, mint, ginger, cocoa powder, and mayonnaise into a blender or food processor and process until smooth.

2. With the motor running, add the oil in a thin, steady stream.

3. Season with salt and pepper.

4. Pour the vinaigrette over the warm, seared lamb chops and serve immediately.

...with Orange and Coconut Sauce

Makes 4 Servings

This sauce also goes well on chicken, pork, scallops, and shrimp.

4 cooked lamb chops, seared and warm (see recipe on page 90)

½ cup (125 ml) orange juice

1 tablespoon (15 ml/8 g) cornstarch

1 cup (250 ml) coconut milk

¼ cup (60 ml/62 g) almond butter

2 tablespoons (30 ml/42 g) honey

1 tablespoon (15 ml/6 g) grated fresh ginger

Salt and black pepper to taste

1. In a saucepan, whisk the cornstarch into the orange juice to make a slurry.

2. Add the coconut milk, almond butter, honey, and ginger and cook over medium heat, stirring frequently, until the sauce has cleared and thickened.

3. Reduce the heat to low and season with salt and pepper.

4. Pour the sauce over the warm, seared lamb chops and serve immediately.

...with Creamy Mushroom and Mint Sauce

Makes 4 Servings

This sauce also goes well on beef, chicken, duck, white fish, pork, rabbit, salmon, scallops, and shrimp.

4 cooked lamb chops, seared and warm (see recipe on page 90)

2 tablespoons (30 ml/28 g) unsalted butter

8 ounces (225 g) fresh mushrooms, thinly sliced

2 cloves (6 g) peeled garlic, minced or pressed

2 teaspoons (10 ml) flour

½ cup (125 ml) heavy cream

1 tablespoon (15 ml/15 g) prepared Dijon-style mustard

2 tablespoons (30 ml/11 g) chopped fresh spearmint leaves

Salt and black pepper to taste

1. Melt the butter in a skillet over medium heat.

2. Add the mushrooms and cook, stirring frequently, until they're tender and lightly browned.

3. Add the garlic and continue cooking until it's golden brown and fragrant.

4. Stir in the flour and continue to cook, stirring constantly, until it smells toasty and turns a light brown.

5. Add the heavy cream and mustard. Continue cooking, stirring constantly, until the sauce boils and thickens.

6. Reduce the heat to low, stir in the mint, and season with salt and pepper.

7. Spoon the sauce over the warm, seared lamb chops and serve immediately.

Marinated Lamb Chops

Makes 4 Servings

These grilled chops are also great cut into bite-size pieces and used in a spinach salad.

4 (8 ounce/225 g) loin chops

¼ cup (60 ml) vegetable oil

1 small onion, peeled and finely chopped, about ½ cup (70 g)

1 clove (3 g) peeled garlic, minced or pressed

Juice of 1 lemon, about 3 tablespoons (45 ml)

1 teaspoon (5 ml) chopped fresh parsley

1 teaspoon (5 ml/6 g) salt

½ teaspoon (2.5 ml) ground black pepper

1 bay leaf

1. In a skillet over medium heat, heat 2 tablespoons (30 ml) of the oil.

2. Add the onion and cook until it's tender and translucent.

3. Add the garlic and continue to cook until it's golden brown and fragrant.

4. Transfer to a bowl and stir in the lemon juice, parsley, salt, pepper, and remaining oil.

5. Divide the marinade between four heat-stable, resealable pouches. Add a quarter of the bay leaf and one chop to each pouch, squeeze out all the air, and seal. (See instructions page 250.)

6. Refrigerate the pouches for at least 3 hours.

7. When ready to cook, preheat the water bath to 125°F (50°C) for a rare chop, 130°F (55°C) for a medium-rare chop, or 140°F (60°C) for a medium chop.

8. Put the sealed pouches into the preheated water bath and cook them for 1–1½ hours.

Pasteurization: When serving immune compromised individuals, cook 1–1¼ inch (25–30 mm) thick chops for either 2 hours at 130°F (55°C) or 1 hour at 140°F (60°C) to ensure that they're safe for them to eat.

9. About 15 minutes before serving, preheat a gas or charcoal grill until it's very hot.

10. Remove the chops from their pouches and sear them on the very hot grill until they're mahogany brown in color, about one minute per side.

11. Serve immediately.

Roast Rack of Lamb
Makes 4 Servings

1 (2 pound/1 kg) frenched rack of lamb
High-smoke-point oil, such as grapeseed, peanut, or vegetable
Salt and black pepper

1. Preheat the water bath to 125°F (50°C) for rare, 130°F (55°C) for medium-rare, or 140°F (60°C) for medium.

2. Pour just enough oil into a heavy skillet to cover the bottom. Heat the oil over high heat, watching carefully, until it just begins to smoke.

3. Sear all sides of the rack of lamb until lightly browned, about 15–30 seconds per side.

4. Wrap the bones with parchment paper or aluminum foil to prevent them from piercing the pouch and vacuum-seal the rack in a large pouch.

5. Put the sealed pouch into the preheated water bath and cook it for 1–1½ hours.

Pasteurization: When serving immune compromised individuals, cook the rack of lamb for either 2½ hours at 130°F (55°C) or 1½ hour at 140°F (60°C) to ensure that it's safe for them to eat.

6. Remove the rack from its pouch and pat it dry with paper towels.

7. Generously season the lamb with salt and pepper.

8. Pour just enough oil into a heavy skillet to cover the bottom. Heat the oil over high heat, watching carefully, until it just begins to smoke.

9. Sear all sides of the rack until they're a deep mahogany brown, about 30–45 seconds per side.

10. Blot the seared lamb with a paper towel to remove excess oil.

Alternative: The surface can also be browned with a kitchen blowtorch. Hold the blowtorch 4–6 inches (10–15 cm) from the meat and move the flame slowly over the surface until it's mahogany brown in color.

11. Slice the seared rack into chops and serve immediately.

Leg of Lamb
Makes 8–10 Servings

5–6 pound (2–2.5 kg) boneless leg of lamb, lamb chuck roast,
or lamb square-cut shoulder

2–3 tablespoons (30–40 ml) vegetable oil (optional)

Salt and black pepper to taste

1½ cups (375 ml) mint jelly (optional)

1. Preheat the water bath to 130°F (55°C) for medium-rare or 140°F
(60 °C) for medium.

2. Vacuum-seal the lamb in a large vacuum pouch. If the lamb is too large
to fit into a single pouch, divide it into pieces and vacuum-seal each piece
in a separate pouch.

3. Put the sealed pouch(es) into the preheated water bath and cook for
1 day (20–26 hours).

4. To finish, preheat a gas or charcoal grill until it's very hot.

5. Remove the cooked lamb from the pouch(es) and pat the lamb dry with
paper towels.

6. Rub the lamb with oil and generously season it with salt and pepper.

7. Grill each side of the lamb until the surface is a deep mahogany brown,
about two minutes per side.

> *Alternative: The lamb can also be seared in a smoking-hot skillet.*
> *1. Pour just enough high-smoke-point oil into a heavy skillet to cover
> the bottom. Heat the oil over high heat, watching carefully, until it just
> begins to smoke.*
> *2. Sear each side of the lamb until it's a deep mahogany brown,
> about 30–45 seconds per side.*
> *3. After searing, blot the lamb with a paper towel to remove excess oil.*

8. Slice the lamb and serve immediately, say with mint jelly on the side.

Leg of Lamb

...with Onion and Mint Sauce

Makes 8–10 Servings

This sauce also goes well with beef, chicken, duck, pork, rabbit, salmon, shellfish, and striped bass.

5–6 pound (2–2.5 kg) cooked boneless leg of lamb, seared and warm (see recipe on page 98)

2 tablespoons (60 ml) olive oil

1 small onion, peeled and finely chopped, about ½ cup (70 g)

½ teaspoon (2 ml) dried rosemary

½ teaspoon (2 ml) dried thyme

2 cloves (6 g) peeled garlic, minced or pressed

1 cup (250 ml) mint jelly

1 tablespoon (15 ml/6 g) orange zest

1 tablespoon (15 ml) white vinegar

Salt and black pepper to taste

1. In a saucepan, heat the olive oil over medium heat.

2. Add the onion and cook, stirring occasionally, until it's tender and translucent.

3. Add the rosemary, thyme, and garlic. Continue to cook until the garlic is golden brown and fragrant.

4. Add the mint jelly, orange zest, and vinegar. Continue cooking, stirring frequently, until the jelly melts.

5. Reduce the heat to low and season with salt and pepper.

6. Spoon the sauce over the warm, sliced lamb and serve immediately.

...with Eggplant Sauce
Makes 8–10 Servings

5–6 pound (2–2.5 kg) cooked boneless leg of lamb, seared and warm (see recipe on page 98)

2 eggplants, about 2½ pounds (1 kg)

6 tablespoons (90 ml/90 g) tahini, a toasted sesame seed butter

2 cloves (6 g) peeled garlic, minced or pressed

Juice of 2 lemons, about 6 tablespoons (100 ml)

1 teaspoon (5 ml) dried rosemary

½ teaspoon (2 ml) dried thyme

¼ teaspoon (1 ml) cayenne pepper

Salt and black pepper to taste

1. At least 2 hours before serving, preheat an oven to 450°F (225°C).

2. Cut the eggplants in half lengthwise, put them cut side down on an oiled sheet pan, and cook them in the oven until their skin is charred and their interior is fully cooked, about one hour.

3. Remove the eggplants from the oven and let them cool on a wire rack until they can be handled.

4. Scrape the eggplant pulp into a blender or food processor, add the tahini, garlic, lemon juice, rosemary, thyme, and cayenne pepper, and process until it's smooth.

5. Season with salt and pepper.

6. Spoon the sauce onto the plate, top with the warm, sliced lamb, and serve immediately.

> *Tip: Use the leftover lamb and sauce to make a pita sandwich. Between paper towels, warm two pieces of pita bread at a time by microwaving them for 30–40 seconds on high. Spread ¼ cup (60 ml) sauce on the bottom of each pita, add 6 ounces (170 g) sliced lamb, ½ cup (35 g) shredded iceberg lettuce, and ¼ cup (45 g) diced fresh tomato. Roll the open pita to make a tube and serve.*

Barbecued Lamb Shanks

Makes 4 Servings

4 (1 pound/0.5 kg) lamb shanks

High-smoke-point oil, such as grapeseed, peanut, or vegetable

½ cup (120 ml) barbecue sauce, store-bought or from the recipe on page 88 or 89

1. Preheat the water bath to 175°F (80°C).

2. Pour just enough oil into a heavy skillet to cover the bottom. Heat the oil over high heat, watching carefully, until it just begins to smoke.

3. Sear the lamb shanks until they're lightly browned, about 20–35 seconds per side. Work in batches, if necessary, to avoid overcrowding the skillet.

4. Vacuum-seal each shank in a separate pouch.

5. Put the sealed pouches into the water bath and cook for 12–24 hours.

6. Remove the shanks from the pouches and pat them dry with paper towels.

8. Pour just enough oil into a heavy skillet to cover the bottom. Heat the oil over high heat, watching carefully, until it just begins to smoke.

9. Sear all sides of the rack until they're a deep mahogany brown, about 30–45 seconds per side.

10. Blot the seared lamb with a paper towel to remove excess oil.

11. Immediately serve the cooked shanks topped with the barbecue sauce.

Young Rabbit with Bacon and Sage Gravy

Makes 4 Servings

This gravy also goes well on chicken, duck, white fish, lamb, pork, shrimp, striped bass, trout, turkey, and venison.

1 young wild rabbit, cut into pieces

1 cup (250 ml) water

⅓ cup (80 ml) cider vinegar

1 tablespoon (15 ml/15 g) prepared Dijon-style mustard

¼ teaspoon (1 ml) garlic powder

¼ teaspoon (1 ml) onion salt

High-smoke-point oil, such as grapeseed, peanut, or vegetable

Gravy

3 slices (24 g) bacon, chopped

3 tablespoons (45 ml/24 g) flour

½ teaspoon (2 ml) dried thyme

½ teaspoon (2 ml) dried rubbed sage

2 cups (500 ml) milk

Salt and black pepper to taste

1. Preheat the water bath to 140°F (60°C).

2. In a small bowl, stir together the water, vinegar, mustard, garlic powder, and onion salt.

3. Put each piece of rabbit into a separate resealable pouch and divide the vinegar mixture among the pouches. Squeeze all the air out of the pouches and seal.

4. Put the sealed pouches into the preheated water bath and cook for 2–3 hours.

5. To prepare the gravy:
    1. Cook the bacon in a skillet over medium heat until it's crispy.
    2. Remove the bacon with a slotted spoon and reserve.
    3. Stir the flour, thyme, and sage into the bacon fat and cook until the flour smells toasty and turns a light brown.
    4. Add the milk and continue cooking, stirring constantly, until the sauce has thickened.

5. Reduce the heat to low, stir in the reserved bacon, and season with salt and pepper.

6. Remove the rabbit from the pouches and pat them dry with paper towels.

7. Pour just enough oil into a heavy skillet to cover the bottom. Heat the oil over high heat, watching carefully, until it just begins to smoke.

8. Sear the pieces of rabbit until they're golden brown, about 15–25 seconds per side. Work in batches, if necessary, to avoid over-crowding the skillet.

9. Immediately serve the rabbit topped with the gravy.

Pan-Seared Venison
Makes 4 Servings

2 pounds (1 kg) venison, divided into four 8 ounce (225 g) pieces
Salt and black pepper
High-smoke-point oil, such as grapeseed, peanut, or vegetable

1. Preheat the water bath to 130°F (55°C) for medium-rare or 140°F (60°C) for medium.

2. Vacuum-seal each piece of venison in a separate pouch.

3. Put the sealed pouches into the preheated water bath and cook for 1–1½ hours if it's from the loin region, for 6–8 hours if it's from the rib region, for 12–18 hours if it's from the hip region, or for 1–2 days (24–48 hours) if it's from the shoulder (chuck) or leg region.

4. Remove the pieces of venison from the pouches and pat them dry with paper towels.

5. Generously season with salt and pepper.

6. Pour just enough oil into a heavy skillet to cover the bottom. Heat the oil over high heat, watching carefully, until it just begins to smoke.

7. Sear all sides of the venison until they're a deep mahogany brown, about 15–30 seconds per side. Work in batches, if necessary, to avoid overcrowding the skillet.

8. Serve immediately.

Pan-Seared Venison

...with Juniper Berry Sauce

Makes 4 Servings

2 pounds (1 kg) cooked venison, seared and warm (see recipe on page 104)

¼ cup (60 ml) cognac

1 cup (250 ml) chicken stock

2 teaspoons (10 ml) dried juniper berries

1 tablespoon (15 ml) red currant jelly

¼ teaspoon (1 ml) dried thyme

½ cup (125 ml) heavy cream

Salt and black pepper to taste

1. After searing the venison, put it on a warm platter and tent it with aluminum foil.

2. Pour the excess oil out of the skillet used to sear the venison and add the cognac before returning it to the cooktop.

3. Heat the cognac over medium heat and scrape the brown bits off the bottom of the pan.

4. When the pan is almost dry, add the stock, juniper berries, currant jelly, and thyme. Continue to cook, stirring frequently, until the liquid has reduced by about half.

5. Add the cream and continue cooking until the sauce has reduced and thickened.

6. Season with salt and pepper.

7. Pour the sauce over the venison and serve immediately.

Pan-Seared Venison

...with Apple and Pear Sauce

Makes 4 Servings

This sauce also goes well on chicken and pork.

2 pounds (1 kg) cooked venison, seared and warm
(see recipe on page 104)

2 tablespoons (30 ml/28 g) unsalted butter

1 small onion, peeled and finely chopped, about ½ cup (70 g)

1 apple, peeled and diced, about 1½ cups (160 g)

1 pear, peeled and diced, about 1 cup (160 g)

1 tablespoon (15 ml/8 g) flour

1 cup (250 ml) milk

¼ cup (60 ml/40 g) raisins

Salt and black pepper to taste

1. About 30 minutes before serving, melt the butter in a skillet over medium heat.

2. Add the onion and cook, stirring frequently, until it's tender and translucent.

3. Add the apple and pear, and continue to cook until they've softened.

4. Stir in the flour and continue cooking until it smells toasty and turns a light brown.

5. Add the milk and raisins, and continue to cook, stirring occasionally, until the sauce has thickened.

6. Reduce the heat to low and season with salt and pepper.

7. Pour the sauce over the warm, seared venison and serve immediately.

Pan-Seared Venison

...with Mustard and Caper Sauce

Makes 4 Servings

This sauce is also great on beef, chicken, white fish, lamb, pork, rabbit, salmon, and shellfish.

2 pounds (1 kg) cooked venison, seared and warm
(see recipe on page 104)

2 tablespoons (30 ml) vegetable oil

1 small onion, peeled and finely chopped, about ½ cup (70 g)

1 shallot, peeled and finely chopped

¼ cup (60 ml) beef stock

¼ cup (60 ml/58 g) sour cream

1 tablespoon (15 ml/15 g) prepared Dijon-style mustard

2 tablespoons (30 ml) balsamic vinegar

2 tablespoons (30 ml/1.7 g) small capers, drained

2 tablespoons (30 ml/8 g) chopped fresh parsley

Salt and black pepper to taste

1. Heat the oil in a skillet over medium heat.

2. Add the onion and shallot, and cook, stirring frequently, until they're tender and translucent.

3. Stir in the stock, sour cream, mustard, vinegar, and capers. Continue to cook, stirring frequently, until the sauce is heated through.

4. Reduce the heat to low, stir in the parsley, and season with salt and pepper.

5. Spoon the sauce over the warm, seared venison and serve immediately.

Pan-Seared Venison

...with Bacon and Swiss Cheese Sauce

Makes 4 Servings

This sauce also goes well on beef, chicken, duck, white fish, lamb, rabbit, salmon, sea bass, shellfish, and turkey.

2 pounds (1 kg) cooked venison, seared and warm
(see recipe on page 104)

2 tablespoons (30 ml/28 g) unsalted butter

¼ cup (125 ml/40 g) peeled and chopped shallot

2 ounces (55 g) fresh specialty mushrooms,[3] thinly sliced

1 tablespoon (15 ml/8 g) flour

1 ounce (28 g) fresh baby spinach, about 1 cup

1 cup (250 ml) milk

2 ounces (57 g) shredded Swiss cheese

2 slices (16 g) bacon, chopped and cooked

1 tablespoon (15 ml) lemon juice

Salt and black pepper to taste

1. Melt the butter in a skillet over medium heat.

2. Add the shallot and mushrooms, and cook, stirring frequently, until they're tender and the shallot is translucent.

3. Stir in the flour and continue to cook until it smells toasty and turns a light brown.

4. Add the spinach and continue cooking, stirring frequently, until it's wilted.

5. Stir in the milk and Swiss cheese. Continue to cook, stirring frequently, until the sauce has thickened and the cheese has melted.

6. Reduce the heat to low, stir in the bacon and lemon juice, and season with salt and pepper.

7. Spoon the sauce over the warm, seared venison and serve immediately.

---

[3] Good choices include: chanterelle, crimini, morel, portabella, and shiitake. If using shiitake mushrooms, discard the stems.

Pan-Seared Venison

...with Cream and Wine Sauce

Makes 4 Servings

This sauce is also great on beef, grouper, pork, and trout.

**2 pounds (1 kg) cooked venison, seared and warm
(see recipe on page 104)**

1 clove (3 g) peeled garlic, minced or pressed

½ cup (125 ml) white wine

4 ounces (110 g) cream cheese with herbs

½ cup (125 ml) heavy cream

⅛ teaspoon (0.5 ml) cayenne pepper

Salt and black pepper to taste

1. After searing the venison, put it onto a warm platter and tent it with aluminum foil.

2. Pour most of the oil from the skillet used to sear the venison, leaving only about 1–2 tablespoons (15–30 ml), and place it over medium heat.

3. Add the garlic and cook until it's golden brown and fragrant.

4. Add the wine and scrape the brown bits off the bottom of the pan.

5. When the pan is almost dry, add the cream cheese, cream, and cayenne pepper. Continue to cook, stirring constantly, until it's heated through.

6. Reduce the heat to low and season it with salt and pepper.

7. Pour the sauce over the warm, seared venison and serve immediately.

Pan-Seared Venison
...with Bacon and Mushroom Sauce
Makes 4 Servings

This sauce also goes well on beef, cod, grouper, lamb, and salmon.

**2 pounds (1 kg) cooked venison, seared and warm
(see recipe on page 104)**

4 slices (32 g) bacon, chopped

4 ounces (110 g) fresh mushrooms, thinly sliced

1 clove (3 g) peeled garlic, minced or pressed

2 tablespoons (30 ml/16 g) flour

1 cup (250 ml) chicken stock

½ cup (125 ml) red wine

1 tablespoon (15 ml/4 g) chopped fresh parsley

Salt and black pepper to taste

1. In a skillet over medium heat, cook the bacon until it's crispy.

2. Remove the bacon with a slotted spoon and reserve.

3. Pour most of the bacon fat from the pan, leaving only about 1–2 tablespoons (15–30 ml).

4. Add the mushrooms and cook, stirring frequently, until they're tender and lightly browned.

5. Add the garlic and continue to cook until it's golden brown and fragrant.

6. Stir in the flour and continue cooking until it's toasty and lightly browned.

7. Add the stock and continue to cook, stirring frequently, until the sauce has thickened.

8. Reduce the heat to low and cover until needed.

9. After searing the venison in a separate skillet, pour off the oil.

10. Reduce the heat to medium and add the wine to the skillet used to sear the venison. Cook, stirring constantly, until the liquid has reduced by about half.

11. Add the mushroom sauce to the reduced wine, stir in the reserved bacon and parsley, and season with salt and pepper.

12. Spoon the sauce over the venison and serve immediately.

Poultry & Eggs

T oday's poultry, like today's meat, is leaner and younger than ever before. Which is why traditional cooking methods often produce dry and tasteless poultry. With sous vide cooking, you can cook poultry so that it's plump, juicy, and very safe.

Doneness & Food Safety

Cooking poultry and meat are very similar. Both lean poultry and lean meat are only plump and juicy if they never exceed 140–150°F (60–65°C)— the temperature at which the muscle fibers shrink (lengthwise) and squeeze out the natural juices. Tougher (and fattier) cuts of meat and poultry can be cooked to higher temperatures and remain juicy, because the melted fat lubricates the lean meat.

Traditional cooking methods make poultry safe by cooking the coldest part to 165°F (74°C) or above. Poultry can also be made safe at lower temperatures, it just takes longer. Indeed, cooking chicken and turkey breasts at 140°F (60°C), as described in the following recipes, is just as safe as cooking them to 165°F (74°C).

Lean poultry meat, such as chicken and turkey breast, is moist, plump, and juicy when cooked at 140°F (60°C) and duck breasts are delicious pasteurized at 135°F (57°C). Dark poultry meat, such as legs and thighs, is best cooked well done at 160–175°F (70–80°C) until it's fall-apart tender.

Searing & Crispy Skin

Searing skinless chicken breasts is challenging—it is very easy to overcook the interior while searing the exterior to a beautiful golden brown. The faster you're able to sear the chicken breast, the less overcooked the interior will be. A heavy skillet with smoking-hot oil can sear one side of a chicken breast to a golden brown in about 15–25 seconds—which is fast enough to keep the interior plump and juicy. If you aren't comfortable searing your chicken breast in a skillet with smoking-hot oil, you can use a skillet with shimmering oil if you speed up the browning reaction by applying a corn-syrup-and-water wash to the chicken breast.

Getting crispy skin on a poultry breast is even more challenging. If the skin is left on the breast, it will absorb too much liquid while it cooks and won't get crispy. Trying to brown the soggy skin (while still on the breast) will cause the water it absorbed to steam the breast until it's dry and stringy. The easiest way to get crispy skin is to remove it before cooking and crisp it in the oven between sheet pans while the breasts cook sous vide—this method also works great with salmon skin. (See discussion on the next page.)

Pan-Seared Chicken Breasts

Makes 4 Servings

You will need a pair of sheet pans and parchment paper to crisp the skin.

4 (6 ounce/170 g) boneless chicken breasts, thawed or frozen
High-smoke-point oil, such as grapeseed, peanut, or vegetable
Salt and black pepper to taste

1. Preheat the water bath to 140°F (60°C).

   Tip: If you like crispy skin, remove it before vacuum-sealing breast.
   1. Preheat the oven to 350°F (175°C).
   2. Cover a rimmed sheet pan with parchment paper.
   3. Lay the skin in a single layer on the parchment paper covered sheet pan.
   4. Cover the skin with another sheet of parchment paper and another sheet pan.
   5. Put the sheet pans into the oven and cook until the skin is a deep golden brown, about 20–30 minutes.
   6. Remove the sheet pans from the oven and transfer the crispy skin to a wire rack to cool. Be cautious of the hot rendered fat in the bottom sheet pan.

2. Vacuum-seal each chicken breast in a separate pouch. Since pulling a strong vacuum on a thawed chicken breast can make it taste dry, press the "stop and seal" button when you see the edges of the breast starting to be squeezed by the pouch. (If you're using a chamber vacuum-sealer, use a 90–95% vacuum.)

3. Put the sealed pouches into the preheated water bath and cook the chicken for at least 2 hours (or 3 hours from frozen).

   Freezing: Since reheating is quicker than cooking, it's often convenient to cook a large batch and freeze them—just make sure the pouches are fully submerged and do not overlap when cooking. The cooked chicken breasts can be frozen for up to a year.
   1. Put the sealed pouches into an ice water bath that's at least half ice for about 30 minutes.
   2. Dry the pouches off with a towel and put them into a freezer.
   3. To reheat the chicken, put the frozen pouches into a preheated 140°F (60°C) water bath for about 45 minutes.

4. Remove the chicken breasts from their pouches and pat them dry with paper towels. Pull the skin off the breast and discard, if present.

5. Pour just enough oil into a heavy skillet to cover the bottom. Heat the oil over high heat, watching carefully, until it just begins to smoke.

6. Sear only one side of the breasts until it's golden brown, about 15–25 seconds. Work in batches, if necessary, to avoid overcrowding the pan.

7. Remove the chicken from the pan and blot them with a paper towel to remove excess oil.

Alternative: You can sear the breasts in shimmering (rather than smoking-hot) oil if you first brush the chicken with a corn-syrup-and-water wash.
1. In a small bowl, stir about ½ teaspoon (2 ml) light corn syrup into about ¼ cup (60 ml) water until thoroughly mixed.
2. Using a pastry brush, brush the surface of the breasts with the corn syrup mixture.
3. In a skillet, heat the oil over medium-high heat until it's shimmering. Then sear the breasts on only one side until golden brown, about 15–25 seconds. Work in batches, if necessary, to avoid overcrowding the skillet.

8. Season the chicken with salt and pepper. Serve immediately.

Pan-Seared Chicken Breasts

...with Rosemary and Mushroom Sauce

Makes 4 Servings

This sauce also goes well with beef, duck, white fish, lamb, pork, salmon, turkey, and venison.

4 cooked boneless, skinless chicken breasts, seared and warm (see recipe on page 113)

2 tablespoons (30 ml) vegetable oil

8 ounces (225 g) fresh mushrooms, thinly sliced

1 clove (3 g) peeled garlic, minced or pressed

1 tablespoon (15 ml/8 g) flour

1 cup (250 ml) chicken stock

Juice of 1 lemon, about 3 tablespoons (45 ml)

1 teaspoon (5 ml) fresh rosemary or ½ teaspoon (2 ml) dried

2 tablespoons (30 ml/8 g) chopped fresh parsley

Salt and black pepper to taste

1. Heat the oil in a skillet over medium heat until shimmering.

2. Add the mushrooms and cook until they're tender and lightly browned.

3. Add the garlic and continue to cook until it's golden brown and fragrant.

4. Stir in the flour and continue cooking, stirring constantly, until it smells toasty and turns a light brown

5. Stir in the stock, lemon juice, and rosemary and continue to cook, stirring frequently, until it's thickened.

6. Stir in the parsley and season with salt and pepper.

7. Spoon the sauce over the warm, cooked chicken and serve immediately.

Pan-Seared Chicken Breasts

...with Creamy Leek and Corn Sauce

Makes 4 Servings

This sauce also goes well with beef, trout, and salmon.

**4 cooked boneless, skinless chicken breasts, seared and warm
(see recipe on page 113)**

2 tablespoons (30 ml/28 g) unsalted butter

1 small onion, peeled and finely chopped, about ½ cup (70 g)

1 cup (250 ml/90 g) chopped leeks, white and light green part only

½ cup (125 ml/40 g) corn kernels, fresh or frozen

1½ tablespoon (20 ml/12 g) flour

⅔ cup (150 ml) chicken stock

⅓ cup (75 ml) heavy cream

2 teaspoons (10 ml) white vinegar

¼ teaspoon (1 ml) ground nutmeg

Salt and black pepper to taste

1. Melt the butter in a saucepan over medium heat.

2. Add the onion and cook, stirring occasionally, until it starts to soften.

3. Add the leeks and corn. Continue to cook, stirring frequently, until the leeks and onion are tender and translucent.

4. Stir in the flour and continue cooking until it smells toasty and turns a light brown.

5. Stir in the stock, cream, vinegar, and nutmeg, and continue to cook, stirring frequently, until thickened.

6. Reduce the heat to low, season with salt and pepper, and cover until ready to serve.

7. Pour the sauce over the warm, cooked chicken and serve immediately.

Pan-Seared Chicken Breasts

...with Peach Salsa

Makes 4 Servings

This salsa also goes well on duck.

4 cooked boneless, skinless chicken breasts, seared and warm
(see recipe on page 113)

1 cup (250 ml/150 g) diced ripe peaches

¼ cup (60 ml/40 g) peeled and chopped yellow onion

1–2 jalapeño chiles, seeded and chopped, about 1½ tablespoons (20 g)

1 tablespoon (15 ml/6 g) grated fresh ginger

Juice of ½ a lime, about 1 tablespoon (15 ml)

1 tablespoon (15 ml) balsamic vinegar

Salt and black pepper to taste

1. Stir the peaches, onion, chiles, ginger, lime, and vinegar together in a bowl.

2. Season with salt and pepper.

3. Cover and refrigerate until needed.

4. Spoon the salsa over the warm, cooked chicken and serve immediately.

Pan-Seared Chicken Breasts

...with Creamy Spinach and Bacon Sauce

Makes 4 Servings

This sauce also goes well with beef, duck, white fish, ham, lamb, salmon, and venison.

4 cooked boneless, skinless chicken breasts, seared and warm (see recipe on page 113)

8 ounces (225 g) frozen chopped spinach, cooked and drained, reserving ¼ cup (60 ml) of the cooking liquid

½ cup (125 ml) half-and-half

2 slices (16 g) bacon, chopped

2 clove (6 g) peeled garlic, minced or pressed

2 teaspoons (10 ml) white vinegar

Salt and black pepper to taste

1. Put the cooked spinach and half-and-half into a blender and process until smooth.

2. In a skillet over medium heat, cook the bacon until it's crispy. Remove the bacon with a slotted spoon and reserve.

3. Add the garlic and cook until it's fragrant and golden brown.

4. Stir in the reserved spinach cooking liquid and the vinegar.

5. Add the spinach mixture and continue to cook, stirring frequently, until the sauce is heated through.

6. Stir in the reserved bacon and season with salt and pepper.

7. Reduce the heat to low and cover until ready to serve.

8. Pour the sauce over the warm, cooked chicken and serve immediately.

Pan-Seared Chicken Breasts

...with Lemon and Almond-Butter Cream Sauce

Makes 4 Servings

This sauce also goes well on white fish, lamb, pork, and venison.

4 cooked boneless, skinless chicken breasts, seared and warm (see recipe on page 113)

¾ cup (175 ml) heavy cream

¼ cup (60 ml/63 g) almond butter

2 teaspoons (10 ml/14 g) honey

¼ teaspoon (1 ml) dried rosemary

Juice of 1 lemon, about 3 tablespoons (45 ml)

Salt and black pepper to taste

1. In a saucepan over medium heat, whisk together the cream, almond butter, honey, and rosemary until well blended.

2. Cook, stirring frequently, until heated through.

3. Stir in the lemon juice and season with salt and pepper.

4. Reduce the heat to low and cover until you're ready to serve.

5. Spoon the sauce over the warm, cooked chicken and serve immediately.

Pan-Seared Chicken Breasts

...with Avocado and Mango Salsa

Makes 4 Servings

This salsa is also great on tropical fish and pork.

4 cooked boneless, skinless chicken breasts, seared and warm (see recipe on page 113)

2 ripe avocados, seeded, peeled, and diced, about 1¾ cups (270 g)

1 ripe mango, peeled, seeded, and diced, about 1¼ cups (200 g)

1 cup (250 ml/165 g) diced fresh pineapple

½ small red onion, peeled and finely chopped, about ¼ cup (35 g)

2 jalapeño chiles, seeded and chopped, about 2 tablespoons (30 g)

2 tablespoons (30 ml) lime juice

2 teaspoons (10 ml/4 g) orange zest

Salt and black pepper to taste

1. Combine the avocados, mango, pineapple, onion, chiles, lime juice, and orange zest together in a bowl.

2. Season with salt and pepper.

3. Cover and refrigerate until needed.

4. Spoon the salsa over the warm, cooked chicken and serve immediately.

Pan-Seared Chicken Breasts
...Teriyaki

Makes 4 Servings

This sauce also goes well with beef, duck, white fish, pork, salmon, turkey, and venison.

4 cooked boneless, skinless chicken breasts, seared and warm (see recipe on page 113)

¼ cup (125 ml) soy sauce

1 tablespoon (15 ml/8 g) cornstarch

¼ cup (60 ml) mirin, a sweetened Japanese rice wine

¼ cup (60 ml) sake

2 tablespoons (30 ml/25 g) granulated sugar

1 clove (3 g) peeled garlic, minced or pressed

1 teaspoon (5 ml/2 g) grated fresh ginger

1. Whisk the cornstarch into the soy sauce to make a slurry.

2. In a saucepan, combine the soy sauce slurry, mirin, sake, sugar, garlic, and ginger, and cook over medium heat, stirring frequently, until it's cleared and thickened.

3. Reduce the heat to low until ready to serve.

4. Pour the sauce over the warm, cooked chicken and serve immediately.

Pan-Seared Chicken Breasts

...with Creamy Wine Sauce

Makes 4 Servings

This sauce also goes well with beef, pork, and trout.

**4 cooked boneless, skinless chicken breasts, seared and warm
(see recipe on page 113)**

3 slices (24 g) bacon, chopped

8 ounces (225 g) fresh mushrooms, thinly sliced

1 clove (3 g) peeled garlic, minced or pressed

1 cup (250 ml) dry white wine

½ cup (125 ml/115 g) sour cream

Sugar, salt, and black pepper to taste

1. In a skillet over medium heat, cook the bacon until it's crispy. Remove the bacon with a slotted spoon and reserve.

2. Add the mushrooms and cook, stirring frequently, until they're tender and lightly browned.

3. Add the garlic and continue to cook until it's golden brown and fragrant.

4. Add the wine, bring to a boil, and continue cooking until it's reduced by half.

5. Stir in the sour cream and continue to cook until the sauce is heated through.

6. Stir in the reserved bacon and season with sugar, salt, and pepper.

7. Reduce the heat to low and cover until you're ready to serve.

8. Pour the sauce over the warm, cooked chicken and serve immediately.

Pan-Seared Chicken Breasts

...with Honey and Poppy-Seed Sauce

Makes 4 Servings

This sauce also goes well with beef, duck, lamb, pork, sea bass, shellfish, and venison.

4 cooked boneless, skinless chicken breasts, seared and warm (see recipe on page 113)

¼ cup (60 ml/85 g) honey

¼ cup (60 ml/115 g) sour cream

½ teaspoon (2 ml) poppy seeds

½ teaspoon (2 ml) grated fresh ginger

Juice of 1 lemon, about 3 tablespoons (45 ml)

Salt and black pepper to taste

1. In a small bowl, stir the honey, sour cream, poppy seeds, ginger, and lemon juice together until smooth.

2. Season with salt and pepper.

3. Spoon the sauce over the warm, cooked chicken and serve immediately.

Pan-Seared Chicken Breasts

...with Orange and Grape Sauce

Makes 4 Servings

This sauce also goes well with duck, lamb, and pork.

**4 cooked boneless, skinless chicken breasts, seared and warm
(see recipe on page 113)**

½ cup (125 ml) orange juice

1 tablespoon (15 ml/8 g) cornstarch

½ cup (125 ml) dry white wine

1 tablespoon (15 ml/21 g) honey

1 teaspoon (5 ml) dried rosemary

1 cup (250 ml/150 g) seedless grapes, each cut in half

1 tablespoon (15 ml/3 g) chopped fresh spearmint leaves

Salt and black pepper to taste

1. In a saucepan, whisk the cornstarch into the orange juice to make a slurry. Then whisk the wine, honey, and rosemary into the slurry.

2. Cook over medium heat, stirring frequently, until the sauce has cleared and thickened.

3. Stir in the grapes and continue to cook until they're heated through.

4. Reduce the heat to low, stir in the mint, season with salt and pepper, and cover until ready to serve.

5. Spoon the sauce over the warm, cooked chicken and serve immediately.

...with Creamy Onion and Rosemary Sauce

Makes 4 Servings

This sauce also goes well with beef, white fish, lamb, pork, salmon, and venison.

4 cooked boneless, skinless chicken breasts, seared and warm (see recipe on page 113)

2 tablespoons (30 ml/28 g) unsalted butter

1 small onion, peeled and finely chopped, about ½ cup (70 g)

1 clove (3 g) peeled garlic, minced or pressed

1½ tablespoons (20 ml/12 g) flour

1 cup (250 ml) milk

Juice of 1 lemon, about 3 tablespoons (45 ml)

½ teaspoon (2 ml) dried rosemary

Salt and black pepper to taste

1. Melt the butter in a saucepan over medium heat.

2. Add the onions and cook, stirring occasionally, until tender and translucent.

3. Add the garlic and continue to cook until it's fragrant and golden brown.

4. Stir in the flour and continue cooking, stirring continuously, until it smells toasty and turns a light brown.

5. Stir in the milk, lemon juice, and rosemary, and continue to cook, stirring frequently, until it thickens.

6. Reduce the heat to low, season with salt and pepper, and cover until ready to serve.

7. Pour the sauce over the warm, cooked chicken and serve immediately.

Pan-Seared Chicken Breasts

...with Sesame Vinaigrette

Makes 4 Servings

This sauce also goes well with beef, duck, grouper, pork, and salmon, and makes a great dressing for salad greens.

4 cooked boneless, skinless chicken breasts, seared and warm
(see recipe on page 113)

2 tablespoons (30 ml) rice wine vinegar

2 tablespoons (30 ml) soy sauce

1 clove (3 g) peeled garlic, minced or pressed

1 teaspoon (5 ml/5 g) mayonnaise

½ cup (125 ml) vegetable oil

¼ cup (60 ml) sesame oil

2 tablespoons (30 ml/12 g) chopped green onions

1 tablespoon (15 ml/8 g) toasted sesame seeds

½ teaspoon (2 ml) red pepper flakes

Salt and black pepper to taste

1. Shortly before serving, put the vinegar, soy sauce, garlic, and mayonnaise into a blender and process until smooth.

2. With the motor running, add the vegetable oil in a thin, steady stream.

3. Transfer to a bowl and slowly add the sesame oil, while whisking vigorously, in a thin stream. (The blender compromises the flavor of sesame oil.)

4. Stir in the green onions, sesame seeds, and red pepper flakes, and season with salt and pepper.

5. Pour the sauce over the warm, cooked chicken and serve immediately.

Pan-Seared Chicken Breasts

...with Orange and Plum Sauce

Makes 4 Servings

This sauce also goes well with duck and pork.

4 cooked boneless, skinless chicken breasts, seared and warm (see recipe on page 113)

¾ **cup (175 ml) orange juice**

1 tablespoon (15 ml/8 g) cornstarch

2 tablespoons (30 ml/42 g) honey

2 tablespoons (30 ml) soy sauce

½ **teaspoon (2 ml) grated fresh ginger**

¼ **teaspoon (1 ml) ground cinnamon**

1 cup (250 ml/165 g) seeded and chopped plums

¼ **cup (60 ml/27 g) blanched (or roasted) almonds, chopped**

Salt and black pepper to taste

1. In a saucepan, whisk the cornstarch into the orange juice to make a slurry.

2. Stir in the honey, soy sauce, ginger, cinnamon, plums, and almonds.

3. Cook over medium heat, stirring frequently, until the sauce has cleared and thickened.

4. Reduce the heat to low, season with salt and pepper, and cover until you're ready to serve.

6. Spoon the sauce over the warm, cooked chicken and serve immediately.

Pan-Seared Chicken Breasts

...with Goat Cheese and Sun-Dried Tomato Relish

Makes 4 Servings

This relish also makes a delicious topping for bruschetta.

4 cooked boneless, skinless chicken breasts, seared and warm
(see recipe on page 113)

2 tablespoons (30 ml) extra virgin olive oil

1 clove (3 g) peeled garlic, minced or pressed

6 sun-dried tomato halves, rehydrated in boiling water for 15 minutes,
drained, and chopped

1 teaspoon (5 ml) fresh rosemary or ½ teaspoon (2 ml) dried

1 cup (250 ml/140 g) crumbled goat cheese

Juice of 1 lemon, about 3 tablespoons (45 ml)

Salt and black pepper to taste

1. Heat the oil in a small saucepan over medium heat.
2. Add the garlic and cook until it's golden brown and fragrant.
3. Transfer the garlic and oil to a bowl.
4. Stir in the sun-dried tomatoes, rosemary, goat cheese, and lemon juice.
5. Season with salt and pepper.
6. Spoon the relish over the warm, cooked chicken and serve immediately.

...with Carrot and Onion Sauce

Makes 4 Servings

This sauce also goes well on beef, duck, white fish, lamb, pork, salmon, trout, turkey, and venison.

4 cooked boneless, skinless chicken breasts, seared and warm (see recipe on page 113)

2 tablespoons (30 ml/28 g) unsalted butter

1 small onion, peeled and finely chopped, about ½ cup (70 g)

½ cup (125 ml/55 g) grated carrot

1 cup (250 ml) chicken stock, room temperature or cooler

1 tablespoon (15 ml/8 g) cornstarch

Juice of 1 lemon, about 3 tablespoons (45 ml)

3 tablespoons (45 ml/38 g) granulated sugar

½ teaspoon (2 ml) dried thyme

1 tablespoon (15 ml/4 g) chopped fresh parsley or cilantro

Salt and black pepper to taste

1. Melt the butter in a saucepan over medium heat.

2. Add the onion and carrots, and cook until they're tender and the onion is translucent.

3. Meanwhile, stir the cornstarch into the stock to make a slurry.

4. Add the stock slurry, lemon juice, sugar, and thyme. Continue cooking, stirring frequently, until the sauce has cleared and thickened.

5. Reduce the heat to low, stir in the parsley, season with salt and pepper, and cover until ready to serve.

6. Spoon the sauce over the warm, cooked chicken and serve immediately.

Pan-Seared Chicken Breasts

...with Lemon and Dill Sauce

Makes 4 Servings

This sauce also goes well with white fish, lamb, and salmon.

4 cooked boneless, skinless chicken breasts, seared and warm
(see recipe on page 113)

2 tablespoons (30 ml/28 g) unsalted butter

8 ounces (225 g) fresh mushrooms, thinly sliced

1 clove (3 g) peeled garlic, minced or pressed

½ teaspoon (2 ml) paprika

1½ tablespoons (20 ml/12 g) flour

1 cup (250 ml) chicken stock

Juice of 1 lemon, about 3 tablespoons (45 ml)

½ teaspoon (2 ml) dried dill weed

½ teaspoon (2 ml) dried thyme

Salt and black pepper to taste

1. In a skillet over medium heat, melt the butter.

2. Add the mushrooms and cook, stirring frequently, until they're tender and lightly browned.

3. Add the garlic and paprika and continue to cook until the garlic is fragrant and golden brown.

4. Stir in the flour and continue cooking, stirring constantly, until it smells toasty and turns a light brown.

5. Add the stock, lemon juice, dill, and thyme, and continue to cook, stirring frequently, until thickened.

6. Reduce the heat to low, season with salt and pepper, and cover until you're ready to serve.

7. Spoon sauce over the warm, cooked chicken and serve immediately.

Pan-Seared Chicken Breasts

Pan-Seared Chicken Breasts
...with Apricot and Orange Sauce
Makes 4 Servings

This sauce also goes well with duck, lamb, and pork.

4 cooked boneless, skinless chicken breasts, seared and warm (see recipe on page 113)

2 tablespoons (30 ml/28 g) unsalted butter

1 small onion, peeled and finely chopped, about ½ cup (70 g)

1 clove (3 g) peeled garlic, minced or pressed

⅔ cup (150 ml/210 g) apricot preserve

⅓ cup (75 ml) orange juice

1 tablespoon (15 ml) white vinegar

1 teaspoon (5 ml) dried rosemary

Salt and black pepper to taste

1. Melt the butter in a skillet over medium heat.

2. Add the onion and cook, stirring occasionally, until it's tender and translucent.

3. Add the garlic and continue to cook until it's fragrant and golden brown.

4. Stir in the apricot preserve, orange juice, vinegar, and rosemary. Continue cooking, stirring constantly, until the sauce is smooth and heated through.

5. Reduce the heat to low, season with salt and pepper, and cover until you're ready to serve.

6. Pour the sauce over the warm, cooked chicken and serve immediately.

Pan-Seared Chicken Breasts

...with Lemon and Saffron Sauce

Makes 4 Servings

This sauce also goes well with beef, fish, lamb, pork, and shellfish.

4 cooked boneless, skinless chicken breasts, seared and warm (see recipe on page 113)

2–4 cups (0.5–1 l/0.3–0.6 kg) cooked basmati rice or cooked couscous

Sauce

⅛ teaspoon (0.5 ml) saffron threads

1 clove (3 g) peeled garlic, minced or pressed

¼ teaspoon (1 ml) anise extract (optional)

1 large egg yolk, pasteurized as on page 164

1 tablespoon (15 ml) lemon juice

1 cup (250 ml) vegetable oil

Salt and black pepper to taste

1. Soak the saffron threads in 1 tablespoon (15 ml) warm water for about 20 minutes.

2. Put the saffron and water, garlic, anise extract, yolk, and lemon juice into a blender or food processor and process until smooth.

3. With the machine running, add the oil in a thin, steady stream.

4. Transfer to a bowl and season with salt and pepper.

5. Spoon the sauce over the warm, cooked chicken and serve immediately with the cooked rice or couscous.

Pan-Seared Chicken Breasts

...Marsala

Makes 4 Servings

This sauce also goes well with beef, duck, fish, lamb, pork, turkey, and venison.

4 cooked boneless, skinless chicken breasts, seared and warm (see recipe on page 113)

2 slices (16 g) pancetta or bacon, chopped

8 ounces (225 g) fresh mushrooms, thinly sliced

1 clove (3 g) peeled garlic, minced or pressed

1 teaspoon (5 ml) tomato paste

1½ cups (375 ml) marsala wine

Juice of 1 lemon, about 3 tablespoons (45 ml)

2 tablespoons (30 ml/28 g) cold unsalted butter

1 tablespoon (15 ml/4 g) chopped fresh parsley

Salt and black pepper to taste

1. In a skillet over medium heat, cook the pancetta (or bacon) until crispy.

2. Remove the pancetta (or bacon) from the skillet with a slotted spoon and reserve.

3. Add the mushrooms to the skillet and cook, stirring frequently, until they're tender and slightly browned.

4. Stir in the garlic and tomato paste and continue to cook until the garlic is golden brown and fragrant.

5. Add the wine, bring to a boil, and continue to cook until it's reduced by half.

6. Stir in the lemon juice and reserved pancetta (or bacon).

7. Reduce the heat to low, whisk in the cold butter, and season with salt and pepper.

8. Pour the sauce over the warm, cooked chicken, sprinkle with the fresh parsley, and serve immediately.

Pan-Seared Chicken Breasts

...Piccata

Makes 4 Servings

This sauce also goes well with beef, white fish, lamb, and pork.

4 cooked boneless, skinless chicken breasts, seared and warm (see recipe on page 113)

1 teaspoon (5 ml) olive oil

1 clove (3 g) peeled garlic, minced or pressed

1 cup (250 ml) chicken stock

Juice of 2 lemons, about 6 tablespoons (90 ml)

2 tablespoons (30 ml/17 g) small capers, drained

2 tablespoons (30 ml/28 g) cold unsalted butter

1 tablespoon (15 ml/4 g) chopped fresh parsley

Salt and black pepper to taste

1. Heat the olive oil in a saucepan over medium heat.

2. Add the garlic and cook until it's fragrant and golden brown.

3. Add the stock, lemon juice, and capers. Continue to cook, stirring frequently, until the sauce has reduced and thickened enough to coat the back of a spoon.

4. Remove from the heat and whisk in the cold butter.

5. Stir in the parsley and season with salt and pepper.

6. Spoon the sauce over the warm, cooked chicken and serve immediately.

Tandoori Chicken

Makes 4 Servings

4 (6 ounce/170 g) boneless, skinless chicken breasts

4 cups (1 l/630 g) cooked basmati rice

Marinade

1 cup (250 ml) plain yogurt

2 teaspoons (10 ml/4 g) curry powder

2 cloves (6 g) peeled garlic, minced or pressed

2 teaspoons (10 ml/4 g) grated fresh ginger

1 teaspoon (5 ml/2 g) paprika

½ teaspoon (2 ml) chili powder

Salt and cayenne pepper to taste

1. Preheat the water bath to 140°F (60°C).

2. To make the marinade:
   1. In a small bowl, mix the yogurt, curry powder, garlic, ginger, paprika, and chili powder together until it's smooth.
   2. Season with salt and pepper.

3. Divide the marinade among four heat-stable, resealable pouches. Add a chicken breast to each pouch, squeeze out all the air, and seal. (See discussion page 250.)

4. Put the sealed pouches into the water bath and cook for at least 2 hours.

5. Remove the breasts from their pouches and reserve the sauce that has formed in the pouch.

6. Grill the breasts on a hot grill (or grill-pan) until grill marks form, about 1–2 minutes.

7. Remove from the grill, top with a little reserved sauce, and serve immediately with the cooked rice.

Chicken with Pineapple and Orange Sauce

Makes 4 Servings

The sauce in this recipe also goes well with pork.

4 (6 ounce/170 g) boneless, skinless chicken breasts

High-smoke-point oil, such as grapeseed, peanut, or vegetable

Marinade

1 tablespoon (15 ml/6 g) orange zest

1 teaspoon (5 ml/3 g) garlic powder

¼ cup (60 ml) barbecue sauce, store-bought
or from the recipe on page 88 or 89

Sauce

1½ cup (375 ml/375 g) canned crushed pineapple in pineapple juice, not drained

⅓ cup (75 ml) orange juice

1 tablespoon (15 ml/8 g) cornstarch

1 tablespoon (15 ml/21 g) honey

2 teaspoons (10 ml/4 g) grated fresh ginger

½ teaspoon (2 ml) onion powder

1 tablespoon (15 ml/3 g) chopped fresh spearmint leaves

Salt and black pepper to taste

1. To prepare the marinade, mix the orange zest, garlic powder, and barbecue sauce together in a small bowl.

2. Divide the marinade between four vacuum pouches, and vacuum-seal a chicken breast in each pouch.

3. Return the chicken breasts to the refrigerator to marinate for at least 1–2 hours.

4. Preheat the water bath to 140°F (60°C).

5. Put the sealed pouches into the preheated water bath and cook for at least 2 hours.

6. To prepare the sauce:

   1. Whisk the pineapple, orange juice, cornstarch, honey, ginger, and onion powder together in a saucepan.

2. Cook over medium heat, stirring frequently, until the sauce has cleared and thickened.

3. Stir in the mint and season with salt and pepper.

4. Turn the heat down to low and cover until ready to serve.

7. Remove the chicken breasts from their pouches and pat them dry with paper towels.

8. Pour just enough oil into a heavy skillet to cover the bottom. Heat the oil over high heat, watching carefully, until it just begins to smoke.

9. Sear the breasts on only one side until nicely browned, about 15–25 seconds. Work in batches, if necessary, to avoid overcrowding the skillet.

10. Pour the sauce over the chicken breasts and serve immediately.

Chicken Legs

Makes 4 Servings.

4 chicken legs (drumstick and thigh), with or without skin
Salt and black pepper
4 tablespoons (60 ml/60 g) unsalted butter
High-smoke-point oil, such as grapeseed, peanut, or vegetable

1. Preheat the water bath to 175°F (80°C).

2. Generously season the chicken with salt and pepper.

3. Vacuum-seal each leg in a separate pouch with 1 tablespoon (15 g) of butter.

4. Put the sealed pouches into the preheated water bath and cook for 4–6 hours.

5. Once the legs have finished cooking, remove the pouches from the bath and let them cool on the counter for about 15 minutes.

> *Freezing: The cooked chicken legs can be frozen for up to a year.*
> *1. Put the sealed pouches into an ice water bath that's at least half ice for at about an hour, adding ice as needed.*
> *2. Dry the pouches off with a towel and put them into a freezer.*
> *3. To reheat the chicken, put the frozen pouches into a preheated 140°F (60°C) water bath for about 45 minutes.*

6. Remove the legs from the pouches and pat them dry with paper towels.

7. Pour just enough oil into a heavy skillet to cover the bottom. Heat the oil over high heat, watching carefully, until it just begins to smoke.

8. Put the legs into the skillet, working in batches if necessary, and sear both sides until golden brown, about 15–25 seconds per side. Blot the seared legs with a paper towel to remove excess oil.

> *Alternative: You can also sear the legs under the broiler.*
> *1. Position an oven rack so the top of the chicken legs will be 4–6 inches (10–15 cm) from the broiler.*
> *2. Preheat the broiler until it is very hot.*
> *3. Put the legs on a wire rack over a foil covered sheet pan.*
> *4. Broil the legs until they're golden brown, about 1–2 minutes.*

9. Serve immediately.

Chicken Legs

...with Orange Barbecue Sauce

Makes 4 Servings

This sauce also goes well with beef, duck, lamb, and pork.

4 cooked chicken legs, seared and warm (see recipe on page 138)

⅓ cup (75 ml/110 g) orange marmalade

⅔ cup (150 ml) tomato sauce

2 tablespoons (30 ml) white vinegar

2–3 canned chipotle chiles in adobo sauce, rinsed and chopped, about 2 tablespoons (50 g)

1 clove (3 g) peeled garlic, minced or pressed

1 teaspoon (5 ml) ground cumin

½ teaspoon (2 ml) ground coriander

½ teaspoon (2 ml) ground ginger

Salt and black pepper to taste

1. In a saucepan over medium heat, combine the orange marmalade, tomato sauce, vinegar, chiles, garlic, cumin, coriander, and ginger. Cook, stirring frequently, until it comes to a simmer.

2. Reduce the heat to low, season with salt and pepper, and cover until you're ready to serve.

3. Pour the sauce over the warm, cooked chicken legs and serve immediately.

Chicken Legs

...Curried

Makes 4 Servings

This sauce also goes well beef, salmon, and venison. For variety, consider adding some pineapple, spinach, or lentils.

4 cooked chicken legs, seared, warm, and torn into bite-size pieces (see recipe on page 138)

4 cups (1 l/630 g) cooked basmati rice

Sauce

1 tablespoon (15 ml/14 g) unsalted butter

1 medium apple, peeled and diced, about 1½ cups (160 g)

2 tablespoons (30 ml/20 g) peeled and chopped shallot

2 teaspoons (10 ml/4 g) curry powder

½ cup (125 ml) chicken stock

1 teaspoon (5 ml) tomato paste

¼ cup (60 ml) heavy cream

Salt and black pepper to taste

1. Melt the butter in a saucepan over medium heat.

2. Add the apple, shallot, and curry powder and cook until the shallots are tender and translucent.

3. Stir in the stock and tomato paste, bring to a boil, and continue to cook until the apples are tender.

4. Add the heavy cream, return to a boil, and continue cooking until it's reduced slightly.

5. Reduce the heat to low, season with salt and pepper, and cover until you're ready to serve.

6. Add the bite-size pieces of chicken to the curry sauce, heat through, and serve over the rice.

Turkey Breast with Crispy Skin

Makes 6–8 Servings

You will need a pair of sheet pans and parchment paper to crisp the skin.

1 (3–4 pound/1.5–2 kg) boneless turkey breast
4 tablespoons (60 g) unsalted butter
Salt and black pepper

1. Preheat the water bath to 140°F (60°C).
2. To crisp the skin:

    1. Carefully remove the skin from the turkey breast, generously season it with salt and pepper, and cut it into ¾ inch (20 mm) strips.
    2. Preheat the oven to 350°F (175°C).
    3. Cover a rimmed sheet pan with parchment paper.
    4. Lay the strips in a single layer on the parchment paper covered sheet pan.
    5. Cover the strips with another sheet of parchment paper and another sheet pan.
    6. Put the sheet pans into the oven and cook until the skin is a deep golden brown, about 20–30 minutes.
    7. Remove the sheet pans from the oven and transfer the crispy skin to a wire rack to cool. Be cautious of the hot rendered fat in the bottom sheet pan.

3. Meanwhile, vacuum-seal the breast in a large pouch with the butter.
4. Put the sealed pouch into the preheated water bath and cook for at least 2 ½ hours.

    Freezing: The cooked turkey breast can be frozen for up to a year.
    1. Put the sealed pouch into an ice water bath that's at least half ice for about 45 minutes.
    2. Dry the pouch off with a towel and put it into a freezer.
    3. To reheat the turkey, put the frozen pouch into a preheated 140°F (60°C) water bath for about an hour.

6. Remove the turkey breast from its pouch, slice it, and serve it topped with the crispy skin.

...Mole

Makes 6–8 Servings

This mole sauce is also great on chicken.

1 cooked boneless, skinless turkey breast, sliced and warm
(see recipe on page 141)

2 tablespoons (30 ml) vegetable oil

6 dried and seeded chiles, preferably a mix of mulato, ancho, pasilla,
guajillo, and chipotle chiles, about 100 g

1 small onion, peeled and finely chopped, about ½ cup (70 g)

1 clove (3 g) peeled garlic, minced or pressed

1 tablespoon (15 ml/9 g) toasted sesame seeds

¼ teaspoon (1 ml) ground cinnamon

¼ teaspoon (1 ml) ground coriander

⅛ teaspoon (0.5 ml) ground cloves

1 can (14½ ounce/412 g) diced tomatoes, drained

¼ cup (60 ml/45 g) blanched (or roasted) almonds, chopped

¼ cup (60 ml/55 g) roasted unsalted pepitas (pumpkin or squash seeds)

½ teaspoon (2 ml) dried oregano

2 teaspoons (10 ml/8 g) granulated sugar

1 cup (250 ml) chicken stock

¼ cup (60 ml/35 g) golden raisins

1 ounce (28 g) unsweetened chocolate, chopped

Sherry vinegar to taste

Salt and black pepper to taste

1. Heat the oil in a skillet over medium heat.

2. Add the dried chiles and onion and cook, stirring frequently, until the
onion is tender and translucent.

3. Add the garlic, sesame seeds, cinnamon, coriander, and cloves and
continue to cook until the garlic is golden brown and the spices are
fragrant.

4. In a blender, combine the onion mixture, tomatoes, almonds, seeds,
oregano, sugar, stock, and raisins. Process until the sauce is smooth.

5. Pour into a saucepan and cook over medium heat until heated through.

6. Add the chocolate and continue cooking, stirring constantly, until it's reduced and thickened.

7. Season with vinegar, salt, and pepper.

8. Reduce the heat to low and cover until you're ready to serve.

9. Pour the sauce over the warm, sliced turkey and serve immediately.

...with Apple, Squash, and Onion Sauce
Makes 6–8 Servings

This sauce also goes well with duck, pork, and venison.

1 cooked boneless, skinless turkey breast, sliced and warm
(see recipe on page 141)

2 tablespoons (30 ml/28 g) unsalted butter

1 small onion, peeled and finely chopped, about ½ cup (70 g)

1 pinch baking soda

2 cups (500 ml/250 g) cubed (½ inch/15 mm) winter squash

1 large apple, peeled and diced, about 2 cups (220 g)

⅓ cup (75 ml) apple juice

¼ cup (60 ml/55 g) packed brown sugar

½ teaspoon (2 ml) ground cinnamon

¼ teaspoon (1 ml) dried rubbed sage

¼ teaspoon (1 ml) ground nutmeg

Salt and black pepper to taste

1. Melt the butter in a saucepan over medium heat.

2. Add the onion and cook until it's tender and translucent.

3. Add the baking soda and continue cooking until the onion is golden brown.

4. Add the squash, apple, apple juice, brown sugar, cinnamon, sage, and nutmeg. Bring to a boil and continue to cook, stirring occasionally, until both the squash and the apple are tender.

5. Reduce the heat to low, season with salt and pepper, and cover until you're ready to serve.

6. Spoon the sauce over the warm, sliced turkey and serve immediately.

...with Mushroom and Sun-Dried Tomato Cream Sauce

Makes 6–8 Servings

This sauce is also great on chicken, lamb, pork, salmon, and shrimp.

1 cooked boneless, skinless turkey breast, sliced and warm (see recipe on page 141)

2 tablespoons (30 ml/28 g) unsalted butter

1 small shallot, peeled and finely chopped

8 ounces (225 g) fresh mushrooms, thinly sliced

1 clove (3 g) peeled garlic, minced or pressed

¼ teaspoon (1 ml) ground cumin

⅛ teaspoon (0.5 ml) ground nutmeg

1 cup (250 ml) chicken stock

5 sun-dried tomato halves, rehydrated in boiling water for 15 minutes, drained, and chopped

2 cups (500 ml) heavy cream

¼ cup (60 ml) dry white wine

1 tablespoon (15 ml/4 g) chopped fresh parsley

Salt and black pepper to taste

1. Melt butter in a saucepan over medium heat.

2. Add the shallot and mushrooms and cook, stirring frequently, until the shallot is tender and translucent.

3. Add the garlic, cumin, and nutmeg and continue to cook until the garlic is golden brown and the spices are fragrant.

4. Add the stock, bring to a boil, and continue cooking, stirring occasionally, until the liquid has reduced by half.

5. Add the tomatoes, heavy cream, and wine. Return to a boil and continue to cook, stirring constantly, until it's reduced and thickened.

6. Reduce the heat to low, stir in the parsley, season with salt and pepper, and cover until you're ready to serve.

7. Pour the sauce over the warm, sliced turkey and serve immediately.

...Moroccan

Makes 6–8 Servings

This sauce also goes well on chicken, lamb, and pork.

1 cooked boneless, skinless turkey breast, sliced and warm
(see recipe on page 141)

2 tablespoons (30 ml) vegetable oil

1 large onion, peeled and finely chopped, about 1 cup (150 g)

1 clove (3 g) peeled garlic, minced or pressed

1 teaspoon (5 ml/3 g) ground cinnamon

½ teaspoon (2 ml) cardamom

¼ teaspoon (1 ml) ground cumin

1 pinch saffron threads

Juice of ½ a lemon, about 1½ tablespoons (25 ml)

2 tablespoons (30 ml/8 g) chopped fresh parsley

¼ cup (60 ml/150 g) blanched (or roasted) almonds, chopped

Salt and black pepper to taste

1. Begin soaking the saffron threads in 1 tablespoon (15 ml) warm water for about 20 minutes.

2. Heat the oil in a skillet over medium heat.

3. Add the onion and cook, stirring frequently, until it's tender and translucent.

4. Add the garlic, cinnamon, cardamom, and cumin. Continue to cook until the garlic is golden brown and the spices are fragrant.

5. Transfer the onion mixture to a blender. Add the saffron and water, lemon juice, parsley, and almonds to the blender and process until smooth.

6. If the sauce is too thick, with the motor running, add water one tablespoon (15 ml) at a time until your desired consistency is reached.

7. Transfer the sauce to a bowl and season with salt and pepper.

8. Spoon the sauce over the warm, sliced turkey and serve immediately.

Turkey Breast

...with Oysters, Leeks, and Mushrooms

Makes 6–8 Servings

This sauce also goes well on beef, chicken, white fish, lamb, rabbit, salmon, shellfish, and trout.

1 cooked boneless, skinless turkey breast, sliced and warm
(see recipe on page 141)

3 cups (750 ml) heavy cream

2 tablespoons (30 ml/28 g) unsalted butter

1 medium shallot, peeled and finely chopped

1 medium leek (white and light green part only), washed and chopped, about 1 cup (90 g)

8 ounces (225 g) fresh specialty mushrooms,[4] thinly sliced

1 clove (3 g) peeled garlic, minced or pressed

1 can (10 ounces/284 g) oysters, drained

1 tablespoon (15 ml) champagne vinegar

Salt and black pepper to taste

1. In a saucepan over medium heat, bring the cream to a boil and reduce it by half. Remove it from the heat and set it aside until needed.

2. Melt the butter in a skillet over medium heat.

3. Add the shallot, leek, and mushrooms and cook, stirring occasionally, until everything has softened.

4. Add the garlic and oysters. Continue to cook until the garlic is golden brown and the oysters begin to curl.

5. Stir in the vinegar and reserved cream.

6. Reduce the heat to low, season with salt and pepper, and cover until you're ready to serve.

7. Pour the sauce over the warm, sliced turkey and serve immediately.

---

4 Good choices include: chanterelle, crimini, morel, portabella, and shiitake. If using shiitake mushrooms, discard the stems.

Turkey Breast

...with Tarragon and Mustard

Makes 6–8 Servings

This sauce also goes well on chicken, white fish, lamb, and shrimp.

1 cooked boneless, skinless turkey breast, sliced and warm
(see recipe on page 141)

1 tablespoons (15 ml) extra virgin olive oil

1 clove (3 g) peeled garlic, minced or pressed

½ cup (125 ml/122 g) plain yogurt

2 tablespoons (30 ml/30 g) prepared Dijon-style mustard

1 teaspoon (5 ml/2 g) dried ground tarragon

¼ teaspoon (1 ml) granulated sugar

Salt and black pepper to taste

1. Heat the olive oil and garlic in a saucepan over medium heat until the garlic is golden brown and fragrant.

2. Stir in the yogurt, mustard, tarragon, and sugar and cook, stirring frequently, until heated through.

3. Reduce the heat to low, season with salt and pepper, and cover until you're ready to serve.

4. Spoon the sauce over the warm, sliced turkey and serve immediately.

...with Chipotle Sauce

Makes 6–8 Servings

This sauce is also great on chicken, pork, and shrimp.

1 cooked boneless, skinless turkey breast, sliced and warm
(see recipe on page 141)

1 cup (250 ml/245 g) plain yogurt

¼ cup (60 ml/25 g) chopped green onions

2-3 canned chipotle chiles in adobo sauce, rinsed and chopped

¼ cup (60 ml/65 g) creamy peanut butter

½ can (14½ ounce/412 g) diced tomatoes, drained

Salt and black pepper to taste

1. Put the yogurt, green onions, chiles, and peanut butter into a blender or food processor and process until smooth.

2. Transfer to a saucepan, stir in the tomatoes, and cook over medium heat until it's heated through.

3. Reduce the heat to low, season with salt and pepper, and cover until you're ready to serve.

4. Pour the sauce over the warm, sliced turkey and serve immediately.

Turkey Breast

...with Cranberry and Orange Sauce

Makes 6–8 Servings

This sauce also goes well on chicken, pork, and venison.

**1 cooked boneless, skinless turkey breast, sliced and warm
(see recipe on page 141)**

**Zest and juice of 1 orange, about ½ cup (125 ml) of juice and
1½ tablespoon (20 ml) of zest**

12 ounces (340 g) fresh cranberries

1 cup (250 ml/200 g) granulated sugar

½ teaspoon (2 ml) ground ginger

1 pinch salt

1. In a saucepan, combine the orange juice and zest, cranberries, sugar, ginger, and salt. Bring the mixture to a boil over high heat.

2. Reduce the heat to low and simmer until about half the cranberries have popped open and the sauce has thickened.

3. Transfer to a bowl and cover until needed.

4. Spoon the sauce over the warm, sliced turkey and serve immediately.

Turkey Breast

...with Tomato and Ginger Chutney

Makes 6–8 Servings

This sauce also goes well on beef, chicken, duck, white fish, lamb, pork, rabbit, salmon, shellfish, and venison.

1 cooked boneless, skinless turkey breast, sliced and warm
(see recipe on page 141)

1 can (14½ ounce/412 g) diced tomatoes, drained

2 medium shallots, peeled and chopped

2 tablespoons (30 ml/12 g) grated fresh ginger

⅔ cup (150 ml/135 g) granulated sugar

⅓ cup (80 ml) cider vinegar

¼ teaspoon (1 ml) red pepper flakes

Salt and black pepper to taste

1. In a blender or food processor, process the tomatoes, shallots, ginger, sugar, vinegar, and red pepper flakes until it's smooth.

2. Transfer the mixture to a saucepan and cook over medium heat until it's heated through.

3. Reduce the heat to low, season with salt and pepper, and cover until you're ready to serve.

4 Spoon the chutney over the warm, sliced turkey and serve immediately.

Turkey Legs

Makes 4 Servings

2 (4–5 pound/1.8–2.3 kg) turkey leg quarters

4 tablespoons (60 ml/60 g) unsalted butter

Salt and black pepper

High-smoke-point oil, such as grapeseed, peanut, or vegetable

1. Preheat the water bath to 175°F (80°C).

2. Generously season the legs with salt and pepper. Vacuum-seal each leg in a separate pouch with 2 tablespoons (30 g) of butter.

3. Put the sealed pouches into the preheated water bath and cook for 8–12 hours.

4. When the legs have finished cooking, remove the pouches from the bath and let them cool on the counter for about 15 minutes.

> *Freezing:The cooked turkey legs can be frozen for up to a year.*
> *1. Put the sealed pouches into an ice water bath that's at least half ice for about 1½ hours.*
> *2. Dry the pouches off with a towel and put them into a freezer.*
> *3. To reheat the turkey, put the frozen pouches into a preheated 140°F (60°C) water bath for about 45 minutes.*

5. Remove the legs from the pouches and pat them dry with paper towels.

6. Pour just enough oil into a heavy skillet to cover the bottom. Heat the oil over high heat, watching carefully, until it just begins to smoke.

7. Sear each side of the leg quarters until it is golden brown, about 15–25 seconds per side. Work in batches, if necessary, to avoid over-crowding the skillet.

8. Blot with a paper towel to remove excess oil.

9. Remove the bones, slice and serve immediately.

> *Variation: After removing the legs from their pouches, tear the meat into bite-size pieces; discard the bones and sinew. Then fry the pieces in hot oil until browned.*
> *1. Pour about 3 inches (7–8 cm) vegetable oil into a heavy saucepan (or electric fryer) that's at least twice as high as the oil.*
> *2. Heat the oil to 375°F (190°C).*
> *3. Working in small batches, fry the bite-size turkey pieces until they're nicely brown.*
> *4. Remove the browned turkey pieces from the oil with a large slotted spoon or skimmer and put them on a folded paper towel.*
> *5. Serve immediately.*

Turkey Legs

...with Orange Sauce

Makes 4 Servings

This sauce is also great on beef, chicken, duck, pork, rabbit, salmon, shellfish, and venison.

2 cooked turkey legs, seared and warm (see recipe on page 152)

2 tablespoons (30 ml/28 g) unsalted butter

1 medium onion, peeled and finely chopped, about ¾ cup (110 g)

1 cup (250 ml) orange juice

1 tablespoon (15 ml/8 g) cornstarch

2 tablespoons (30 ml) soy sauce

2 tablespoons (30 ml/28 g) packed brown sugar

2 tablespoons (30 ml/8 g) chopped fresh parsley

½ teaspoon (2 ml) ground ginger

Salt and black pepper to taste

1. Melt the butter in a skillet over medium heat.

2. Add the onion and cook, stirring frequently, until it's tender and translucent.

3. Whisk the cornstarch into the orange juice to make a slurry.

4. Add the orange juice slurry, soy sauce, sugar, parsley, and ginger to the skillet. Continue to cook, stirring occasionally, until the sauce has cleared and thickened.

5. Reduce the heat to low, season with salt and pepper, and cover until you're ready to serve.

6. Spoon the sauce over the warm, sliced turkey and serve immediately.

Duck Breasts

Makes 4 Servings

You will need a pair of sheet pans and parchment paper to crisp the skin.

4 (6 ounce/170 g) boneless duck breasts, skin removed and reserved

Salt and black pepper to taste

1. Preheat the water bath to 135°F (57°C).

2. Vacuum-seal each skinless breast in a separate pouch.

3. Put the sealed pouches into the preheated water bath and cook for 2½–3 hours.

> *Freezing: The cooked duck breasts can be frozen for up to a year.*
> *1. Put the sealed pouches into an ice water bath that's at least half ice for about 30 minutes.*
> *2. Dry the pouches off with a towel and put them into a freezer.*
> *3. To reheat the duck, put the frozen pouches into a preheated 135°F (57°C) water bath for about 45 minutes.*

4. Meanwhile, to crisp the skin:
   1. Preheat the oven to 350°F (175°C).
   2. Cover a rimmed sheet pan with parchment paper.
   3. Lay the skin of each breast in a single layer on the parchment paper covered sheet pan.
   4. Generously season the skin with salt and pepper.
   5. Cover the skin with another sheet of parchment paper and another sheet pan.
   6. Put the sheet pans into the oven and cook until the skin is a deep golden brown, about 20–30 minutes.
   7. Remove the sheet pans from the oven, being careful not to spill the rendered duck fat.
   8. Reserve the fat for future recipes and cool the skin on a wire rack until needed.

5. Remove the breasts from their pouches and pat them dry with paper towels.

6. Cut the breast into ½ inch (15 mm) slices, garnish with the crispy skin, and serve immediately.

Duck Breasts

...with Turnip Sauce

Makes 4 Servings

This sauce is also great on beef, chicken, lamb, pork, and scallops.

4 cooked, boneless, skinless duck breasts, warm (see recipe on page 154)

2 medium turnips, peeled, about 2 cups (240 g)

3 tablespoons (45 ml/43 g) unsalted butter

1 medium shallot, peeled and finely chopped

3 tablespoons (45 ml/23 g) flour

2 cups (500 ml) milk

¼ cup (60 ml/24 g) chopped green onions

¼ cup (60 ml/15 g) chopped fresh parsley

Salt and black pepper to taste

1. About an hour before serving, bring a large pot of water to a boil.

2. Add the turnips and cook them until they're easily pierced with a paring knife, about 30–40 minutes.

3. Remove the cooked turnips from the pot and let them cool until needed.

4. Melt the butter in a large saucepan over medium heat.

5. Add the chopped shallot and cook, stirring frequently, until the shallot is tender and translucent.

6. Stir in flour and continue to cook until the flour is fragrant and slightly browned.

7. Add the milk and continue cooking, stirring occasionally, until thickened.

8. Cut the cooked turnips into ½ inch (15 mm) cubes and add them to the sauce.

9. Stir in the green onions and parsley. Continue cooking until the turnips are heated through.

10. Season with salt and pepper.

11. Spoon the sauce over the warm, cooked duck, garnish with with the crispy skin, and serve immediately.

Duck Breasts

...with Sweet Potato and Apple Relish

Makes 4 Servings

This sauce is also great on chicken, pork, shrimp, and venison.

4 cooked, boneless, skinless duck breasts, warm (see recipe on page 154)

1 medium sweet potato, peeled and cubed, about 1 cup (130 g)

4 tablespoons (60 ml/57 g) unsalted butter

1 medium onion, peeled and finely chopped, about ¾ cup (110 g)

1 large apple, peeled and diced, about 1¾ cups (200 g)

4 ounces (115 g) fresh mushrooms, thinly sliced

Salt and black pepper to taste

1. About 40 minutes before serving, bring a large pot of water to a boil.

2. Add the sweet potato and cook until it's easily pierced with a paring knife, about 20 minutes. Transfer the cooked sweet potato to bowl until needed and discard the cooking water.

3. Melt the butter in a skillet over medium heat.

4. Add the onion and cook until it's tender and translucent.

5. Add the apple and continue to cook, stirring frequently, until it's tender and the onion is golden brown.

6. Add the mushrooms and continue cooking until they've softened.

7. Add the sweet potato to the skillet and continue to cook until it's heated through.

8. Season with salt and pepper.

9. Spoon the relish onto the plates, put a duck breast on the relish, garnish with the crispy skin, and serve immediately.

Duck Legs
Makes 4 Servings

4 (8 ounce/225 g) duck leg quarters
Salt and black pepper
High-smoke-point oil, such as grapeseed, peanut, or vegetable

1. Preheat the water bath to 175°F (80°C).

2. Vacuum-seal each leg in a separate pouch.

3. Put the sealed pouches into the preheated water bath and cook for 8–12 hours.

4. When the legs have finished cooking, remove the pouches from the bath and let them cool on the counter for about 15 minutes.

Freezing: The cooked duck legs can be frozen for up to a year.
1. Put the sealed pouches into an ice water bath that's at least half ice for about an hour.
2. Dry the pouches off with a towel and put them into a freezer.
3. To reheat the duck, put the frozen pouches into a preheated 140°F (60°C) water bath for about 45 minutes.

5. Remove the duck legs from their pouches and pat them dry with paper towels.

6. Generously season with salt and pepper.

7. Pour just enough oil into a heavy skillet to cover the bottom. Heat the oil over high heat, watching carefully, until it just begins to smoke.

8. Sear the legs until they're golden brown, about 15–25 seconds per side. Work in batches, if necessary, to avoid overcrowding the skillet.

9. Serve immediately.

Variation: After removing the legs from their pouches, tear the meat into bite-size pieces; discard the bones and sinew. Then fry the pieces in hot oil until browned.
1. Pour about 3 inches (7–8 cm) vegetable oil into a heavy saucepan (or electric fryer) that's at least twice as high as the oil.
2. Heat the oil to 375°F (190°C).
3. Working in small batches, fry the bite-size duck pieces until they're nicely brown, about 20–30 seconds.
4. Remove the browned duck pieces from the oil with a large slotted spoon or skimmer and put them on a folded paper towel.
5. Serve immediately.

...with Sauerkraut, Apple, and Onion Sauce

Makes 4 Servings

This sauce is also great on pork.

4 cooked duck leg quarters, seared and warm (see recipe on page 157)

4 tablespoons (60 ml/57 g) unsalted butter

1 cup (250 ml/140 g) canned sauerkraut, drained, rinsed well under running water, and excess liquid squeezed out

1 medium apple, peeled and diced, about 1½ cups (160 g)

1 small onion, peeled and finely chopped, about ½ cup (70 g)

2 tablespoons (30 ml/28 g) unsalted butter

2 tablespoons (30 ml/16 g) flour

2 cups (250 ml) chicken stock

Salt and black pepper to taste

1. Melt 4 tablespoons (60 ml) of butter in a large saucepan over medium-low heat.

2. Add the sauerkraut, apple, and onion. Cook, stirring frequently, until the onion and apple are very tender. Transfer the mixture to a bowl and cover until needed.

3. Turn the heat up to medium and melt 2 tablespoons (30 ml) of butter in the pan.

4. Stir in the flour and cook until it smells toasty and turns a light brown.

5. Add the stock and continue to cook, stirring frequently, until thickened.

6. Stir in the sauerkraut mixture and continue cooking until it's heated through.

7. Season with salt and pepper.

8. Spoon the sauce over the warm, seared duck legs and serve immediately.

Duck Leg Confit with Bacon and Mushroom Risotto
Makes 4 Servings

4 (8 ounce/225 g) duck leg quarters

1 quart (1 l) cold water

¼ cup (75 g) table salt

1 stalk fresh rosemary

1 stalk fresh thyme

2 bay leaves

High-smoke-point oil, such as grapeseed, peanut, or vegetable

Risotto

2 slices (16 g) bacon, chopped

8 ounces (225 g) fresh specialty mushrooms,[5] thinly sliced

1 clove (3 g) peeled garlic, minced or pressed

1 cup (250 ml/200 g) arborio or carnaroli rice

¼ cup (60 ml) dry red wine

2½ cups (625 ml) chicken stock

½ cup (125 ml/30 g) finely grated Parmesan cheese

Salt and black pepper to taste

1. To brine the duck legs:
   1. In a large container, make a brine by stirring the salt into the cold water until it dissolves completely.
   2. Add the duck legs, rosemary, thyme, and bay leaves to the brine.
   3. Cover and refrigerate for 1–2 days (24–48 hours).

2. When you're ready to cook the duck, preheat the water bath to 175°F (80°C).

3. Rinse each duck leg under cold running water to remove excess salt.

4. Vacuum-seal each leg in a separate pouch.

5. Put the sealed pouches into the preheated water bath and cook for 8–10 hours.

6. Start preparing the risotto about 30 minutes before serving:

---

5 Good choices include: chanterelle, crimini, morel, portabella, and shiitake. If using shiitake mushrooms, discard the stems.

1. Cook the bacon in a large saucepan over medium heat until crispy.
2. Remove the cooked bacon with a slotted spoon and reserve.
3. Add the mushrooms and continue to cook, stirring frequently, until they're tender and lightly browned.
4. Add the garlic and continue cooking until it's golden brown and fragrant.
5. Stir in the rice and continue to cook until it smells toasty.
6. Add the wine and about a third of the stock. Continue cooking, stirring constantly, until the liquid is absorbed.
7. Add another third of the stock and continue to cook, stirring constantly, until the liquid is absorbed.
8. Add the rest of the stock and continue cooking, stirring constantly, until the risotto is creamy and the rice is fully cooked.
9. Remove from the heat while you sear the duck legs.

7. Remove the duck legs from their pouches and pat them dry with paper towels.

8. Pour just enough oil into a heavy skillet to cover the bottom. Heat the oil over high heat, watching carefully, until it just begins to smoke.

9. Sear the legs until they're golden brown, about 15–25 seconds per side. Work in batches, if necessary, to avoid overcrowding the skillet.

10. Vigorously stir the cheese into the risotto over low heat until well blended.

11. Stir in the reserved bacon and season with salt and pepper.

12. Divide the risotto among four plates, top with a duck leg, and serve immediately.

The 'Perfect' Egg

This "perfect" egg has a custardy texture and can be used in any recipe that calls for a poached egg.

1–12 Large eggs

1. Preheat the water bath to 148°F (64.5°C). For a runny yolk, set the water bath to 145°F (63°C).

2. Put the egg(s), in their shells, into the water bath for 45–60 minutes.

3. Remove the egg(s) from the bath, crack open, and serve immediately.

> *Alternative: For a firmer egg white, the egg(s) can be cooked in a 167°F (75°C) water bath.*
>
> *1. Preheat the water bath to 167°F (75°C).*
> *2. Measure the circumference of the egg(s).*
> *3. Gently put the egg(s) into the water (with a soup ladle) and cook for the time listed in The Perfect Egg Timetable on the next page.*
> *For a runny yolk, you can download a replacement table at http://www.douglasbaldwin.com/sous-vide.html or decrease the cooking time by about 15%.*
> *4. Immediately remove the egg(s) from the water bath, crack open, and serve.*

Circumference (inches)	Time (minutes)	Circumference (cm)	Time (minutes)
2	3	5	3
2¼	3¾	5½	3½
2½	4½	6	4
2¾	5¼	6½	4½
3	6	7	5¼
3¼	7	7¹/₂	5¾
3½	7¾	8	6½
3¾	8¾	8½	7¼
4	10	9	8
4¼	11	9½	8¾
4½	12¼	10	9½
4¾	13½	10½	10½
5	14¾	11	11¼
5¼	16	11½	12¼
5½	17½	12	13¼
5¾	19	12½	14¼
6	20½	13	15¼
6¼	22	13½	16½
6½	23½	14	17½
6¾	25¼	14½	18¾
7	27	15	19¾
7¼	29	15½	21
7½	30¾	16	22¼
7¾	32¾	16½	23½
8	34¾	17	25
		17½	26¼
		18	27¾
		18½	29¼
		19	30¾
		19½	32¼
		20	33¾

Table 1. Cooking time for a perfect soft boiled egg in a 167°F (75°C) water bath based on the egg's circumference.

Hard-Cooked Eggs

Large eggs

1. Preheat the water bath to 167°F (75°C).
2. Put the eggs, in their shells, into the water bath for 45–60 minutes.
3. Remove the egg from the bath.
4. Either remove the shell and serve immediately or refrigerate until needed.

Creamy Scrambled Eggs

Makes 2 Servings

5 large eggs

1 tablespoon (15 ml) heavy cream

1 teaspoon (5 ml) white vinegar

1 pinch sugar

Salt and black pepper to taste

1. Preheat the water bath to 158°F (70°C) or 167°F (75°C).
2. In a bowl, whisk the eggs, cream, vinegar, and sugar together until well mixed.
3. Pour the egg mixture into a heat-stable, resealable pouch. Squeeze out as much air as possible and seal.
4. Put the sealed pouch into the preheated water bath for about an hour at 158°F (70°C) or for about 20 minutes at 167°F (75°C). If cooking at the higher temperature, agitate the pouch every few minutes until it reaches your desired consistency.
5. Pour the scrambled eggs into a bowl, season with salt and pepper, and serve immediately.

Pasteurized in Shell Eggs

Who doesn't love raw cookie dough⁶ or chocolate mousse? Unfortunately, these foods contain raw eggs that can be dangerous to young children, pregnant women, the elderly, or anyone with a compromised immune system. These recipes can be made safer by pasteurizing the eggs first. Pasteurized eggs can be used in any recipe calling for raw eggs—though, the egg whites will be slightly milky and will take longer to whip.

1–12 large eggs

1. Preheat the water bath to 135°F (57°C).

2. Put the eggs, in their shells, into the preheated water bath for at least 1¼ hours (75 minutes).

3. Remove the eggs from the water bath and put them into cold water for 15–20 minutes.

4. Dry the eggs carefully with paper towels and refrigerate them until needed.

---

6 A few studies have found that flour may contain the food pathogens *Salmonella* and *E. coli*. So I recommend buying heat treated flour when making cookie dough that will be eaten raw or undercooked.

Fish & Shellfish

The key to great sous vide fish is to buy only very fresh fish. Fresh fish smells like the sea with a pleasant seaweedy smell. The flesh of fresh fish is shiny, moist, and doesn't pit when pressed with a finger. If buying whole fish, the eyes should look alive (with jet black pupils and crystal clear lenses) and the gills should be bright pink. Fish is highly perishable and should be kept on ice, even in the refrigerator, until you're ready to cook it. Even packed in ice, fish only remains fresh for about a week after being caught. Before going to the market, you may want to check Monterey Bay Aquarium's Seafood Watch for a list of ocean-friendly seafood to be sure you aren't purchasing species that are being overfished or that might have been contaminated with toxic materials.

Fish is cooked to change its texture, develop flavor, and destroy food pathogens. Traditionally, fish is considered to be cooked when it flakes. Fish flakes when the collagen separating the flakes is converted into gelatin at around 115–120°F (46–49°C). This temperature is too low, however, to destroy any food pathogens. So if you prefer your fish cooked rare (108°F/42°C) or medium-rare (120°F/49°C), then you should buy only sushi-grade fish. If you're serving someone who is immune compromised or wouldn't be willing to eat the fish raw, then you should cook the fish to medium (140°F/60°C) and hold it at that temperature until it's been pasteurized.[7] Whatever your temperature preference, sous vide fish retains more healthful omega-3 fatty acids and nutrients than traditionally cooked fish.

---

[7] While the following recipes conform to the FDA's *Fish and Fisheries Products Hazards and Controls Guidance*, it won't reduce viruses like Hepatitis A or norovirus to a safe level. To destroy viruses in shellfish, the US National Advisory Committee on Microbiological Criteria for Foods recommends cooking shellfish until the coldest part is at 194°F (90°C) or above for 90 seconds.

Fish Fillets or Steaks

Makes 4 Servings

1½ pounds (0.7 kg) fish fillets or steaks, skin removed and cut into four 6 ounce (170 g) pieces
Extra virgin olive oil (optional)

1. Preheat the water bath to 140°F (60°C) for medium, 122°F (50°C) for medium-rare, or 108°F (42°C) for rare. Immune compromised individuals should never eat rare or medium-rare fish.

2. Check for and remove any pin-bones from the fillets by using needle-nose pliers or tweezers. You may want to ask your fish monger to remove the skin and pin-bones for you.

> Tip: you can prevent the white film of albumin (a water soluble protein) from coagulating on the surface of your fish by brining it in a 10% salt solution for about 10 minutes.
> 1. Prepare the brine by stirring 1 tablespoon (14 g) table salt into ½ cup (125 ml) cold water until it dissolves completely.
> 2. Put the fish and brine into a resealable pouch, squeeze out the air, and seal.
> 3. Refrigerate for 10 minutes, then remove the fish and rinse it under cold running water to remove excess salt.

3. Vacuum seal each fillet in a separate pouch with, if desired, a few table-spoons (20–30 ml) olive oil. Since pulling a strong vacuum can make the fish taste mushy, press the "stop and seal" button when you see the edges of the fish starting to be squeezed by the pouch. (If you're using a chamber-style vacuum sealer, use a 90–95% vacuum.)

4. Put the sealed pouches into the preheated water bath and cook for 40–50 minutes at 140°F (60°C) or for 15–20 minutes at 108°F (42°C) or 122°F (50°C).

> Freezing: If you cooked your fish at 140°F (60°C), then you can freeze the cooked fish for up to a year.
> 1. Carefully put the sealed pouches into an ice water bath that's at least half ice for about 30 minutes.
> 2. Dry the pouches off with a towel and put them into a freezer.
> 3. To reheat the fish, put the frozen pouches into a preheated 140°F (60°C) water bath for about 30 minutes.

5. Immediately serve, either plain or with your favorite sauce.

> Tip: Serving the fish on warm plates will help rare and medium-rare fish from getting too cold before reaching the table.

Black Sea Bass with Mint Vinaigrette

Makes 4 Servings

This vinaigrette is also great on beef, chicken, duck, halibut, lamb, pork, rabbit, salmon, shellfish, and trout.

1½ pounds (0.7 kg) cooked black sea bass fillets
(see recipe on page 167)

¼ cup (60 ml) sherry vinegar

1 clove (3 g) peeled garlic, minced or pressed

2 tablespoons (30 ml/11 g) chopped fresh spearmint leaves

1 teaspoon (5 ml/5 g) mayonnaise

½ cup (125 ml) vegetable oil

¼ cup (60 ml) extra virgin olive oil

Salt and black pepper to taste

1. Just before serving, put the vinegar, garlic, mint, and mayonnaise into a blender and process until smooth.

2. With the motor running, add the vegetable oil in a thin, steady stream.

3. Transfer the vinaigrette to a bowl and vigorously whisk in the olive oil by hand. (The blender compromises the flavor of extra virgin olive oil.)

4. Season with salt and pepper.

5. Pour the vinaigrette over warm, cooked fish and serve immediately.

Striped Bass with Mushrooms

Makes 4 Servings

This sauce also goes well on beef, chicken, cod, duck, halibut, lamb, pork, rabbit, salmon, shellfish, and venison.

1½ pounds (0.7 kg) cooked striped sea bass fillets
(see recipe on page 167)

2 tablespoons (30 ml) vegetable oil

8 ounces (225 g) fresh mushrooms, thinly sliced

1 shallot, peeled and finely chopped

1 clove (3 g) peeled garlic, minced or pressed

4 tablespoons (60 ml/55 g) unsalted butter

Juice of 1 lemon, about 3 tablespoons (45 ml)

2 tablespoons (30 ml/8 g) chopped fresh parsley, preferably flat-leaf

2 tablespoons (30 ml/6 g) chopped fresh chives

Salt and black pepper to taste

1. About 30 minutes before serving, heat the oil in a skillet over medium-high heat.

2. Add the mushrooms and cook, stirring frequently, until they're tender and lightly browned.

3. Reduce the heat to medium, add the shallot and continue to cook, stirring frequently, until it's tender and translucent.

4. Add the garlic and continue cooking until it's golden brown and fragrant.

5. Stir in the butter and lemon juice until the butter is completely incorporated.

6. Reduce the heat to low and stir in the parsley and chives.

7. Season with salt and pepper.

8. Spoon the sauce over the warm, cooked bass and serve immediately.

Striped Bass with Creamy Red Bell Pepper Sauce

Makes 4 Servings

This sauce is also great on beef, chicken, cod, halibut, lamb, pork, rabbit, and shellfish.

1½ pounds (0.7 kg) cooked striped sea bass fillets
(see recipe on page 167)

3 tablespoons (45 ml/42 g) unsalted butter

1 medium onion, peeled and finely chopped, about ¾ cup (110 g)

2 red or yellow bell peppers, finely chopped, about 1½ cups (240 g)

2 tablespoons (30 ml/16 g) flour

1 cup (250 ml) milk

Juice of ½ a lemon, about 1½ tablespoons (25 ml)

1 teaspoon (5 ml/5 g) prepared Dijon-style mustard

Salt and black pepper to taste

1. About 30 minutes before serving, melt the butter in a skillet over medium heat.

2. Add the onion and bell peppers and cook, stirring occasionally, until both are tender and the onion is translucent.

3. Stir in the flour and continue to cook until it smells toasty and turns a light brown.

4. Stir in the milk, lemon juice, and mustard. Continue cooking, stirring frequently, until the sauce thickens.

5. Reduce the heat to low and season with salt and pepper.

6. Spoon the sauce over the warm, cooked bass and serve immediately.

Cod with Blue Cheese Butter

Makes 4 Servings

This butter is also great on lamb.

1½ pounds (0.7 kg) cooked cod fillets (see recipe on page 167)

6 tablespoons (90 ml/85 g) unsalted butter, room temperature

¼ cup (60 ml/30 g) crumbled blue cheese

1 teaspoon (5 ml) anchovy paste

1 teaspoon (5 ml/5 g) prepared mustard

1 teaspoon (5 ml) white vinegar

½ teaspoon (2 ml) fennel seeds

Salt and black pepper to taste

1. In a small bowl, mix the butter, blue cheese, anchovy paste, mustard, vinegar, and fennel seeds together until smooth.

2. Season with salt and pepper.

3. Cover and refrigerate until you're ready to serve.

4. Serve the warm cod topped with a few tablespoons (20-30 ml) of the butter.

Cod with Potato and Garlic Purée

Makes 4 Servings

This purée also goes well on bass, beef, catfish, chicken, duck, halibut, lamb, pork, rabbit, salmon, scallops, trout, and venison.

1½ pounds (0.7 kg) cooked cod fillets (see recipe on page 167)

1 pound (0.5 kg) red potatoes, peeled and cut into eight pieces

4 cloves (12 g) peeled garlic, minced or pressed

½ cup (125 ml) extra virgin olive oil

¼ cup (60 ml) red wine vinegar

Salt and black pepper to taste

1. At least 45 minutes before serving, put the potatoes into a pot of cold water over medium heat and bring the water to a simmer.

2. Cook the potatoes until they can be easily pierced with a paring knife, about 20–30 minutes.

3. Drain the potatoes and reserve some of the cooking water.

4. Put the cooked potatoes, garlic, olive oil, and vinegar into a blender or food processor and process until smooth.

5. Add the reserved potato cooking water 1 tablespoon (15 ml) at a time until the purée reaches the consistency you prefer.

6. Season with salt and pepper.

7. Spoon the purée onto the plate, top with the warm, cooked cod, and serve immediately.

Fish Fillets or Steaks

Cod with Tomato and White Wine Sauce

Makes 4 Servings

This sauce also goes well on bass, beef, chicken, duck, grouper, halibut, lamb, pork, rabbit, salmon, shellfish, trout, turkey, and venison.

1½ pounds (0.7 kg) cooked cod fillets (see recipe on page 167)

4 cups (1 l/630 g) cooked long-grain white rice

Sauce

2 tablespoons (30 ml/28 g) unsalted butter

1 small onion, peeled and finely chopped, about ½ cup (70 g)

1 clove (3 g) peeled garlic, minced or pressed

1 cup (250 ml) dry white wine

1 can (14½ ounces/412 g) tomato sauce

1 tablespoon (15 ml/4 g) chopped fresh parsley

Salt and black pepper to taste

1. About 30 minutes before serving, melt the butter in a skillet over medium heat.

2. Add the onion and cook, stirring frequently, until it's tender and translucent.

3. Add the garlic and continue to cook until it's golden brown and fragrant.

4. Stir in the wine and bring it to a boil.

5. Add the tomato sauce and continue cooking, stirring frequently, until the sauce reduces and thickens.

6. Reduce the heat to low, stir in the parsley, and season with salt and pepper.

7. To serve, put the warm, cooked fish on a bed of rice and top it with the sauce.

Cod with Lemon and Parsley Sauce

Makes 4 Servings

This sauce also goes well with bass, beef, chicken, duck, grouper, halibut, lamb, pork, rabbit, salmon, shellfish, turkey, and venison.

1½ pounds (0.7 kg) cooked cod fillets (see recipe on page 167)

2 tablespoons (30 ml) olive oil

8 ounces (225 g) fresh mushrooms, thinly sliced

1 clove (3 g) peeled garlic, minced or pressed

Juice of 1 lemon, about 3 tablespoons (45 ml)

¼ cup (60 ml/15 g) chopped fresh parsley, preferably flat-leaf

Salt and black pepper to taste

1. About 30 minutes before serving, heat the oil in a skillet over medium heat.

2. Add the mushrooms and cook until they're tender and lightly browned.

3. Add the garlic and continue to cook until it's golden brown and fragrant.

4. Reduce the heat to low, add the lemon juice, stir in the parsley, and season with salt and pepper.

5. Spoon the sauce over the warm, cooked cod and serve immediately.

Fish Fillets or Steaks

Cod with Caramelized Onions

Makes 4 Servings

This recipe also goes well on bass, beef, chicken, duck, lamb, pork, rabbit, salmon, and venison.

1½ pounds (0.7 kg) cooked cod fillets (see recipe on page 167)

3 tablespoons (45 ml/43 g) unsalted butter

2 medium onions, peeled and sliced, about 2 cups (220 g)

¼ teaspoon (1 ml) baking soda

1 teaspoon (5 ml) tomato paste

2 tablespoons (30 ml) red wine vinegar

Salt and black pepper to taste

1. About 30 minutes before serving, melt the butter in a skillet over medium-low heat.

2. Add the onions and cook, stirring frequently, until they're tender and translucent.

3. Add the baking soda and continue to cook, stirring frequently, until the onions are golden brown.

4. Stir in the tomato paste and continue cooking until it's fragrant.

5. Reduce the heat to low, stir in the vinegar, and season with salt and pepper.

6. Spoon the onions over the warm, cooked cod and serve immediately.

Grouper with Red Bell Pepper Butter

Makes 4 Servings

This butter also goes well on halibut, lamb, pork, sea bass, and trout.

1½ pounds (0.7 kg) cooked grouper fillets (see recipe on page 167)

½ red bell pepper, finely chopped, about ½ cup (60 g)

1 clove (3 g) peeled garlic, minced or pressed

1 teaspoon (5 ml) sherry vinegar

½ teaspoon (2 ml) Tabasco® sauce

¼ teaspoon (1 ml) anchovy paste

8 tablespoons (120 ml/110 g) unsalted butter, cut into pieces

Salt to taste

1. About 30 minutes before serving, put the chopped bell pepper into a steamer. Steam the bell pepper until it's very tender, about 15 minutes.

2. Put the bell pepper, garlic, vinegar, Tabasco sauce, anchovy paste, and butter into a mortar. Crush and grind it with a pestle until it's smooth.

3. Season with salt.

4. Top the warm, cooked grouper with the butter and serve immediately.

Fish Fillets or Steaks

Grouper with Lemon and Caper Sauce

Makes 4 Servings

This sauce also goes well with cod, halibut, lamb, pork, salmon, sea bass, and trout.

1½ pounds (0.7 kg) cooked grouper fillets (see recipe on page 167)

8 tablespoons (120 ml/110 g) unsalted butter

1 small shallot, peeled and finely chopped

¼ cup (60 ml/35 g) small capers, drained

Juice of 1 lemon, about 3 tablespoons (45 ml)

¼ teaspoon (1 ml) anchovy paste

¼ cup (60 ml/15 g) chopped fresh parsley, preferably flat-leaf

Salt and black pepper to taste

1. About 20 minutes before serving, melt 2 tablespoons (30 ml/25 g) of the butter in a skillet over medium-low heat.

2. Add the shallot and cook until it's tender and translucent.

3. Stir in the remaining butter, capers, lemon juice, and anchovy paste. Continue to cook, stirring frequently, until the sauce is smooth.

4. Reduce the heat to low, stir in the parsley, and season with salt and pepper.

5. Spoon the sauce over the warm, cooked grouper and serve immediately.

Haddock with Mushroom and Wine Sauce

Makes 4 Servings

This sauce also goes well with bass, chicken, cod, halibut, lamb, rabbit, salmon, shellfish, and venison.

1½ pounds (0.7 kg) cooked haddock fillets (see recipe on page 167)

2 tablespoons (30 ml/28 g) unsalted butter

1 small shallot, peeled and finely chopped

8 ounces (225 g) fresh mushrooms, thinly sliced

1 clove (3 g) peeled garlic, minced or pressed

1 cup (250 ml) dry white wine

½ teaspoon (2 ml) dried thyme

4 tablespoons (60 ml/56 g) unsalted butter, room temperature

2 tablespoons (30 ml/8 g) chopped fresh parsley, preferably flat-leaf

Salt and black pepper to taste

1. About 45 minutes before serving, melt the butter in a skillet over medium heat.

2. Add the shallot and cook until it's tender and translucent.

3. Add the mushrooms and continue to cook until they're tender and lightly browned.

4. Add the garlic and continue cooking until it's golden brown and fragrant.

5. Stir in the wine and thyme, bring the wine to a boil, and reduce it by at least half.

6. Reduce the heat to low and whisk in the butter.

7. Stir in the parsley and season with salt and pepper.

8. Pour the sauce over the warm, cooked haddock and serve immediately.

Hake with Roasted Red Pepper and Bacon Sauce

Makes 4 Servings

This sauce also goes well with bass, beef, chicken, cod, halibut, lamb, pork, rabbit, shellfish, and trout.

1½ pounds (0.7 kg) cooked hake fillets (see recipe on page 167)

1 jar (12 ounces/340 g) roasted red bell pepper, drained and well rinsed

2 slices (16 g) bacon, chopped

1 shallot, peeled and finely chopped

1 cup (250 ml) chicken stock

2 teaspoons (10 ml) white vinegar

4 tablespoons (60 ml/56 g) unsalted butter, room temperature

Salt and black pepper to taste

1. About 30 minutes before serving, process the roasted red bell peppers in a blender or food processor until they're smooth.

2. In a skillet over medium heat, cook the bacon until it's crispy. Remove the cooked bacon with a slotted spoon and reserve.

3. Add the shallot to the skillet and cook until it's tender and translucent.

4. Add the stock, bring it to a boil, and reduce it by half.

5. Stir in the vinegar and the puréed roasted red bell peppers.

6. Reduce the heat to low and whisk in the butter until it's fully incorporated.

7. Stir in the reserved bacon and season with salt and pepper.

8. Pour the sauce over the warm, cooked hake and serve immediately.

Halibut with Tomato Cream

Makes 4 Servings

This sauce also goes well on lamb, pork, rabbit, salmon, and shellfish.

4 (6 ounce/170 g) cooked halibut steaks (see recipe on page 167)

2 tablespoons (30 ml/28 g) unsalted butter

1 medium onion, peeled and finely chopped, about ¾ cup (110 g)

1 clove (3 g) peeled garlic, minced or pressed

½ cup (125 ml) heavy cream

1 can (14½ ounce/412 g) diced tomatoes, drained

Juice of ½ a lemon, about 1½ tablespoons (25 ml)

¼ teaspoon (1 ml) fennel seeds

Salt and black pepper to taste

1. About 30 minutes before serving, melt the butter in a skillet over medium heat.

2. Add the onion and cook, stirring frequently, until it's tender and translucent.

3. Add the garlic and continue to cook until it's golden brown and fragrant.

4. Stir in the heavy cream and bring it to a boil.

5. Add the tomatoes, lemon juice, and fennel seeds and return to a boil.

6. Reduce the heat to low and season with salt and pepper.

7. Spoon the sauce over the warm, cooked halibut and serve immediately.

Fish Fillets or Steaks

Fish Fillets or Steaks

Halibut with Salsa

Makes 4 Servings

This salsa is also great on bass, chicken, duck, lamb, pork, rabbit, salmon, and shellfish.

4 (6 ounce/170 g) cooked halibut steaks (see recipe on page 167)

2 medium tomatoes, seeded and chopped, about 1½ cups (250 g)

1 small onion, peeled and finely chopped, about ½ cup (70 g)

1 clove (3 g) peeled garlic, minced or pressed

1 jalapeño chile, seeded and chopped, about 1 tablespoon (14 g)

¼ cup (60 ml/4 g) chopped fresh cilantro

2 tablespoons (30 ml/11 g) chopped fresh spearmint leaves

Juice of 1 lime, about 2 tablespoons (30 ml)

Salt and black pepper to taste

1 Mix the tomatoes, onion, garlic, jalapeño pepper, cilantro, mint, and lime together in a bowl.

2. Season with salt and pepper.

3. Cover and refrigerate until needed

4. Spoon the salsa over the warm, cooked halibut and serve immediately.

Mahi-Mahi with Avocado and Melon Salsa

Makes 4 Servings

This salsa also goes well on chicken, scallops, shark, shrimp, and swordfish.

1½ pounds (0.7 kg) cooked mahi-mahi fillet (see recipe on page 167)

1 ripe avocado, seeded, peeled, and diced, about 1⅓ cups (200 g)

1 cup (250 ml/160 g) cubed cantaloupe

1 small red onion, peeled and finely chopped, about ½ cup (70 g)

1 tablespoon (15 ml/4 g) chopped fresh parsley or chopped fresh cilantro

Juice of 1 lemon, about 3 tablespoons (45 ml)

Salt and black pepper to taste

1. In a bowl, mix the avocado, cantaloupe, red onion, parsley (or cilantro), and lemon juice together. Take care not to crush the avocado when mixing.

2. Season with salt and pepper.

3. Use immediately or cover with plastic wrap (pressed directly to the surface of the salsa) and refrigerate until needed.

4. Top the warm, cooked mahi-mahi with the salsa and serve immediately.

Mahi-Mahi with Papaya Salsa

Makes 4 Servings

This salsa also goes well on chicken, scallops, shark, shrimp, and swordfish.

1½ pounds (0.7 kg) cooked mahi-mahi fillet (see recipe on page 167)

1 ripe papaya, diced, about 2 cups (300 g)

1 jalapeño chile, seeded and chopped, about 1 tablespoon (14 g)

1 small red onion, peeled and finely chopped, about ½ cup (70 g)

1 clove (3 g) peeled garlic, minced or pressed

Juice of 1 lemon, about 3 tablespoons (45 ml)

1 tablespoon (15 ml/4 g) chopped fresh cilantro or chopped fresh parsley

Salt and black pepper to taste

1. In a bowl, mix together the papaya, jalapeño pepper, red onion, garlic, lemon juice, and cilantro (or parsley).

2. Season with salt and pepper.

3. Either use immediately or cover and refrigerate until needed.

4. Spoon the salsa over the warm, cooked mahi-mahi and serve immediately.

Mahi-Mahi with Mango Sauce

Makes 4 Servings

This salsa also goes well on chicken, duck, pork, scallops, shark, shrimp, and swordfish.

1½ pounds (0.7 kg) cooked mahi-mahi fillet (see recipe on page 167)

8 tablespoons (120 ml/110 g) unsalted butter

1 small onion, peeled and finely chopped, about ½ cup (70 g)

1 ripe mango, peeled, seeded, and diced, about 1¼ cups (200 g)

2 teaspoons (10 ml/14 g) honey

1 teaspoon (5 ml) balsamic vinegar

Salt and black pepper to taste

1. About 20 minutes before serving, melt about 2 tablespoons (30 ml/25 g) of the butter in a skillet over medium heat.

2. Add the onion and cook, stirring frequently, until it's tender and translucent.

3. Add the remaining butter, mango, honey, and vinegar. Continue cooking, stirring constantly, until the butter is fully incorporated.

4. Remove from the heat and season with salt and pepper.

5. Spoon the sauce over the warm, cooked mahi-mahi and serve immediately.

Pacific Sole with Mushrooms and Tomatoes

Makes 4 Servings

This sauce also goes well on bass, beef, chicken, cod, duck, grouper, halibut, lamb, pork, rabbit, salmon, shellfish, turkey, and venison.

1½ pounds (0.7 kg) cooked Pacific sole fillets (see recipe on page 167)

2 tablespoons (30 ml/28 g) unsalted butter

4 ounces (120 g) fresh mushrooms, thinly sliced

1 clove (3 g) peeled garlic, minced or pressed

1 can (14¼ ounce/412 g) diced tomatoes, drained

Juice of 1 lemon, about 3 tablespoons (45 ml)

½ teaspoon (2 ml) dried thyme

Salt and black pepper to taste

1. About 30 minutes before serving, melt the butter in a skillet over medium high heat.

2. Add the mushrooms and cook, stirring frequently, until they're tender and lightly browned.

3. Reduce the heat to medium, add the garlic and continue to cook until it's golden brown and fragrant.

4. Add the tomatoes, lemon juice, and thyme and continue cooking until the sauce is heated through.

5. Reduce the heat to low and season with salt and pepper.

6. Spoon the sauce over the warm, cooked sole and serve immediately.

Tilapia with Orange Sauce

Makes 4 Servings

This sauce also goes well on chicken, cod, duck, lamb, rabbit, salmon, shellfish, striped bass, turkey, and venison.

1½ pounds (0.7 kg) cooked tilapia fillets (see recipe on page 167)

2 tablespoons (30 ml) vegetable oil

1 small onion, peeled and finely chopped, about ½ cup (70 g)

1 clove (3 g) peeled garlic, minced or pressed

½ cup (125 ml) dry white wine

¼ teaspoon (1 ml) dried thyme

¼ teaspoon (1 ml) dried rosemary

½ cup (125 ml) orange juice

2 teaspoons (10 ml/5 g) cornstarch

Salt and black pepper to taste

1. About 20 minutes before serving, heat the oil in a skillet over medium heat.

2. Add the onion and cook, stirring frequently, until it's tender and translucent.

3. Add the garlic and continue to cook until it's golden brown and fragrant.

4. Stir in the wine, thyme, and rosemary. Bring the wine to a boil and reduce it by at least half.

5. In a small bowl, whisk the cornstarch into the orange juice to make a slurry.

6. Add the orange juice slurry to the skillet and continue cooking, stirring constantly, until the sauce has cleared and thickened.

7. Reduce the heat to low and season with salt and pepper.

8. Pour the sauce over warm, cooked tilapia and serve immediately.

Tilapia with Curry Chutney

Makes 4 Servings

This sauce is also great on chicken and shrimp.

1½ pounds (0.7 kg) cooked tilapia fillets (see recipe on page 167)

½ cup (125 ml/60 g) roasted pistachio nuts

2 tablespoons (30 ml/11 g) chopped fresh spearmint leaves

2 teaspoons (10 ml/4 g) grated fresh ginger

½ cup (125 ml/123 g) plain yogurt

2 teaspoons (10 ml/3 g) curry powder

Juice of 1 lemon, about 3 tablespoons (45 ml)

1 teaspoon (5 ml) vanilla extract

Salt and black pepper to taste

1. Combine the pistachios, mint, ginger, yogurt, curry powder, lemon juice, and vanilla extract in a blender or food processor and process until it's smooth.

2. Transfer to a bowl and season with salt and pepper.

3. Cover and refrigerate until you're ready to serve.

4. Spoon the chutney over the warm, cooked tilapia and serve immediately.

Tilapia with Lemon and Chive Butter

Makes 4 Servings

This butter also goes well on halibut, lamb, pork, rabbit, salmon, and shellfish.

1½ pounds (0.7 kg) cooked tilapia fillets (see recipe on page 167)

6 tablespoons (30 ml/28 g) unsalted butter, room temperature

1 tablespoon (15 ml/3 g) chopped fresh chives

¼ teaspoon (1 ml) fennel seeds

Juice of ½ a lemon, 1½ tablespoons (25 ml)

Salt and black pepper to taste

1. At least 10 minutes before serving, cream the butter, chives, fennel seeds, and lemon juice together until it's smooth.

2. Season with salt and pepper.

3. Divide the butter equally among the warm, cooked fillets and serve immediately.

Fish Fillets or Steaks

Catfish with Avocado and Tomato Sauce

Makes 4 Servings

This sauce is also great with chicken and shellfish..

1½ pounds (0.7 kg) cooked catfish fillets (see recipe on page 167)

½ cup (125 ml) chicken stock, preferably low sodium

2 tablespoons (30 ml) cider vinegar

2 tablespoons (30 ml/30 g) ketchup

1 tablespoon (15 ml) soy sauce

1 tablespoon (15 ml) lemon juice

8 tablespoons (113 g) cold unsalted butter, cut into pieces

Salt and black pepper to taste

1 ripe avocado, about 200 g

1. Combine the vinegar and stock in a saucepan over high heat. Bring to a boil and reduce the liquid to about 1 tablespoon (15 ml).

2. Reduce the heat to low and stir in the ketchup, soy sauce, and lemon juice.

3. Add all the butter and slowly whisk until the sauce is smooth.

4. Season with salt and pepper.

5. Peel, seed and slice the avocado and arrange the slices on the warm, cooked catfish. Spoon the sauce over the catfish and serve immediately.

Cajun Catfish Court Bouillon
Makes 4 Servings

This sauce also goes well with bass, beef, chicken, cod, halibut, lamb, pork, rabbit, shrimp, and trout.

1½ pounds (0.7 kg) cooked catfish fillets (see recipe on page 167)

4 cups (1 l/630 g) cooked long-grain white rice

Sauce

½ cup (125 ml/60 g) flour

½ cup (125 ml) vegetable oil

2 medium onions, peeled and finely chopped, about 1½ cups (220 g)

2 ribs celery, trimmed and finely chopped, about ¾ cup (80 g)

1 medium green bell pepper, finely chopped, about ¾ up (120 g)

2 cloves (6 g) peeled garlic, minced or pressed

1 can (14½ ounce/412 g) diced tomatoes, drained

1 can (6 ounce/170 g) tomato paste

1 cup (250 ml) water

Salt and cayenne pepper to taste

1. About 2 hours before serving, combine the flour and oil in a large saucepan over medium heat. Cook, stirring constantly, until the flour smells toasty and turns a light brown.

2. Add the onions, celery, and bell pepper. Continue to cook, stirring occasionally, until the onions are tender and translucent.

3. Add the garlic and continue cooking until it's fragrant.

4. Add the tomatoes and tomato paste. Continue to cook, stirring frequently, until they're heated through.

5. Reduce the heat to low, add water, and simmer for 1–2 hours.

6. Before serving, season the sauce with salt and cayenne pepper.

7. To serve, put the warm, cooked fish on a bed of rice and top it with the sauce.

> *Variation: For a true court bouillon: place each piece of raw catfish in a heat-stable, resealable pouch; add a ¼ cup (60 ml) of the sauce to each pouch; squeeze the air out of each pouch and seal it; and cook the catfish as described on page 167.*

Mako Shark with Mango and Mint Salsa

Makes 4 Servings

This salsa also goes well on chicken, duck, pork, salmon, and shellfish.

4 (6 ounce/170 g) cooked mako shark steaks (see recipe on page 167)

1 tablespoon (15 ml) olive oil

1 medium onion, peeled and finely chopped, about ¾ cup (110 g)

1 clove (3 g) peeled garlic, minced or pressed

1 ripe mango, peeled, seeded, and diced, about 1¼ cups (200 g)

1 jalapeño chile, seeded and chopped, about 1 tablespoon (14 g)

1 teaspoon (5 ml/2 g) grated fresh ginger

¼ cup (60 ml) orange juice

2 teaspoons (10 ml/6 g) brown sugar

1 tablespoon (15 ml/6 g) chopped fresh spearmint leaves

Salt and black pepper to taste

1. About 30 minutes before serving, heat the oil in a skillet over medium heat.

2. Add the onion and cook, stirring occasionally, until it's tender and translucent.

3. Add the garlic and continue to cook until it's golden brown and fragrant.

4. Reduce the heat to low and add the mango, jalapeño pepper, and ginger. Continue cooking, stirring frequently, until the mango has softened.

5. Add the orange juice and brown sugar. Continue cooking until there is no liquid left in the pan.

6. Transfer the salsa to a bowl and stir in the mint.

7. Season with salt and pepper.

8. Spoon the salsa over the warm, cooked shark and serve immediately.

Sturgeon with Toasted Hazelnuts

Makes 4 Servings

This sauce also goes well on chicken, halibut, rabbit, and sea bass.

1½ pounds (0.7 kg) cooked sturgeon fillets (see recipe on page 167)

4 tablespoons (60 ml/57 g) unsalted butter

1 small shallot, peeled and finely chopped

¼ cup (60 ml/28 g) chopped toasted hazelnuts

2 tablespoons (30 ml/17 g) small capers, drained

Juice of 1 lemon, about 3 tablespoons (45 ml)

2 tablespoons (30 ml/8 g) chopped fresh parsley

Salt and black pepper to taste

1. About 20 minutes before serving, melt the butter in a skillet over medium-low heat.

2. Add the shallot and cook, stirring frequently, until it's tender and translucent.

3. Reduce the heat to low and stir in the hazelnuts, capers, lemon juice, and parsley.

4. Season with salt and pepper.

5. Spoon the sauce over the warm, cooked sturgeon and serve immediately.

Fish Fillets or Steaks

Swordfish with Orange and Star Anise Sauce

Makes 4 Servings

This sauce also goes well on chicken, duck, pork, rabbit, shrimp, and venison.

4 (6 ounce/170 g) cooked swordfish steaks (see recipe on page 167)

2 tablespoons (30 ml/28 g) unsalted butter

2 apples, peeled and diced, about 3 cups (320 g)

1 cup (250 ml) orange juice

1 tablespoon (15 ml/8 g) cornstarch

1 star anise pod or ¼ teaspoon (1 ml) dried anise seeds

¼ teaspoon (1 ml) cayenne pepper

Salt and black pepper to taste

1. About 30 minutes before serving, melt the butter in a skillet over medium heat.

2. Add the apples and cook, stirring frequently, until they're tender and golden brown.

3. In a small bowl, make a slurry by whisking the cornstarch into the orange juice.

4. Add the orange juice slurry, star anise, and cayenne to the skillet. Continue to cook, stirring constantly, until the sauce has cleared and thickened.

5. Reduce the heat to low and season with salt and pepper.

6. Just before serving, remove and discard the star anise pod from the sauce.

7. Spoon the sauce over the warm, cooked swordfish and serve immediately.

Swordfish with Pineapple and Mango Salsa

Makes 4 Servings

This salsa also goes well on chicken, pork, mahi-mahi, salmon, shark, and shellfish.

4 (6 ounce/170 g) cooked swordfish steaks (see recipe on page 167)

1 cup (250 ml/165 g) diced fresh pineapple

½ cup (125 ml/80 g) ripe mangoes, peeled, seeded, and diced

Juice of 1 lime, about 2 tablespoons (30 ml)

1 tablespoon (15 ml/6 g) chopped fresh spearmint leaves (optional)

1 tablespoon (15 ml) chopped fresh cilantro

1 teaspoon (5 ml/2 g) grated fresh ginger

1 jalapeño chile, seeded and chopped, about 1 tablespoon (14 g)

Salt and black pepper to taste

1. In a bowl, combine the pineapple, mangoes, lime juice, mint, cilantro, ginger, and jalapeño pepper.

2. Season with salt and pepper.

3. Cover and refrigerate until you're ready to serve.

4. Top the warm, cooked swordfish with the salsa and serve immediately.

Trout Amandine

Makes 4 Servings

This brown butter sauce is also great on salmon, sea bass, and shellfish.

1½ pounds (0.7 kg) cooked, skinless rainbow trout fillets
(see recipe on page 167)

8 tablespoons (120 ml/110 g) unsalted butter

½ cup (125 ml/55 g) slivered almonds

Juice of 1 lemon, about 3 tablespoons (45 ml)

Salt to taste

1 About five minutes before serving, melt the butter in a skillet over medium heat.

2. Add the almonds and cook, stirring constantly, until the milk solids in the butter are golden brown, about 2–3 minutes.

3. Immediately remove from the heat and stir in the lemon juice.

4. Season with salt.

5. Spoon the sauce over the warm, cooked trout and serve immediately.

Variation: Replace the almonds with ½ cup (125 ml/110 g) chopped pecans and add 1 tablespoon (15 ml/15 g) prepared Dijon-style mustard along with the lemon juice.

Trout with Sherry Browned Butter

Makes 4 Servings

This sauce is also great on salmon, sea bass, and shellfish.

**1½ pounds (0.7 kg) cooked, skinless rainbow trout fillets
(see recipe on page 167)**

8 tablespoons (120 ml/110 g) unsalted butter

1 tablespoon (15 ml) sherry vinegar

Salt to taste

1. About five minutes before serving, melt the butter in a skillet over medium heat.

2. Cook the butter, stirring constantly, until the milk solids are lightly browned, about 2–3 minutes.

3. Immediately remove from the heat and stir in the vinegar.

4. Season with salt.

5. Pour the sauce over the warm, cooked trout and serve immediately.

Trout with Browned Butter and Sage

Makes 4 Servings

This sauce is also great on beef, chicken, cod, duck, grouper, lamb, pork, rabbit, shrimp, striped bass, turkey, and venison.

1½ pounds (0.7 kg) cooked, skinless rainbow trout fillets (see recipe on page 167)

8 tablespoons (110 g) unsalted butter

1 clove (3 g) peeled garlic, minced or pressed

Juice of 1 lemon, about 3 tablespoons (45 ml)

1 teaspoon (5 ml) fresh sage, finely chopped (or ½ teaspoon/2 ml dried rubbed sage)

Salt to taste

1. About five minutes before serving, melt the butter in a skillet over medium heat.

2 Cook the butter, stirring constantly, until the milk solids are golden brown, about 2–3 minutes.

3. Remove from the heat and add the garlic, lemon juice, and sage.

4. Season with salt.

5. Pour the sauce over the warm, cooked trout and serve immediately.

Salmon with Lemon–Mustard Mayonnaise

Makes 4 Servings

This sauce also goes well on chicken, cod, sea bass, and shrimp.

1½ pounds (0.7 kg) cooked salmon fillets (see recipe on page 167)

½ cup (125 ml/118 g) mayonnaise

¼ cup (60 ml) whole milk

2 teaspoons (10 ml/10 g) prepared Dijon-style mustard

Juice of ½ a lemon, about 1½ tablespoons (25 ml)

Salt to taste

1. Stir the mayonnaise, milk, mustard, and lemon juice together.
2. Season with salt, cover, and refrigerate until you're ready to serve.
3. Spoon the sauce over the warm, cooked salmon and serve immediately.

Fish Fillets or Steaks

Salmon with Creamy Onion and Mustard Sauce

Makes 4 Servings

This sauce is also great on beef, chicken, halibut, lamb, shellfish, and striped bass.

1½ pounds (0.7 kg) cooked salmon fillets (see recipe on page 167)

1 medium onion, peeled and finely chopped, about ¾ cup (110 g)

½ cup (125 ml/115 g) sour cream

2 tablespoons (30 ml/30 g) prepared Dijon-style mustard

Juice of 1 lemon, about 3 tablespoons (45 ml)

¼ teaspoon (1 ml) dried dill weed or ½ teaspoon (2 ml) fresh

Salt and black pepper to taste

1. Put the onion into a microwave safe container and microwave it on high until it's tender and translucent, about 2–3 minutes.

2. In a small bowl, combine the onion, sour cream, mustard, lemon juice, and dill together.

3. Season with salt and pepper.

4. Spoon the sauce over the warm, cooked salmon and serve immediately.

Salmon with Red Wine Sauce
Makes 4 Servings

This sauce is also great on beef, cod, grouper, lamb, and venison.

1½ pounds (0.7 kg) cooked salmon fillets (see recipe on page 167)

2 tablespoons (30 g) unsalted butter

1 small shallot, peeled and finely chopped

2 cloves (6 g) peeled garlic, minced or pressed

1 cup (250 ml) red wine

1 cup (250 ml) chicken stock, room temperature or cooler

1 tablespoon (15 ml/8 g) cornstarch

½ teaspoon (2 ml) dried thyme

Salt and black pepper to taste

1. About 40 minutes before serving, melt the butter in a saucepan over medium heat.

2. Add the shallot and cook, stirring frequently, until it's tender and translucent.

3. Add the garlic and continue to cook until it's golden brown and fragrant.

4. Add the wine and continue cooking, stirring occasionally, until the pan is almost dry.

5. In a small bowl, make a slurry by stirring the cornstarch into the stock.

6. Add the stock slurry and thyme and continue to cook, stirring constantly, until the sauce has cleared and thickened.

7. Reduce the heat to low and season with salt and pepper.

8. Pour the sauce over the warm, cooked salmon and serve immediately.

Fish Fillets or Steaks

Salmon with Tomato and Caper Sauce

Makes 4 Servings

This sauce is also great on beef, chicken, cod, halibut, lamb, pork, rabbit, sea bass, and shellfish.

1½ pounds (0.7 kg) cooked salmon fillets (see recipe on page 167)

2 tablespoons (30 ml) olive oil

1 small onion, peeled and finely chopped, about ½ cup (70 g)

1 can (14 ½ ounce/412 g) diced tomatoes, drained

1 clove (3 g) peeled garlic, minced or pressed

3 tablespoons (45 ml/25 g) small capers, drained

1 tablespoon (15 ml/15 g) prepared mustard

¼ cup (60 ml/15 g) chopped fresh parsley, preferably flat-leaf

Juice of 1 lemon, about 3 tablespoons (45 ml)

Salt and black pepper to taste

1. About 30 minutes before serving, heat the oil in a skillet over medium heat.

2. Add the onion and cook, stirring frequently, until it's tender and translucent.

3. Add the garlic and continue to cook until it's golden brown and fragrant.

4. Add the tomatoes, capers, and mustard. Continue cooking, stirring frequently, until the sauce is heated through.

5. Reduce the heat to low and stir in the parsley and lemon juice.

6. Season with salt and pepper.

7. Spoon the sauce over the warm, cooked salmon and serve immediately.

Salmon with Bacon–Balsamic Vinaigrette

Makes 4 Servings

This vinaigrette is also great on beef, chicken, cod, duck, grouper, halibut, lamb, pork, rabbit, shellfish, and venison.

1½ pounds (0.7 kg) cooked salmon fillets (see recipe on page 167)

2 slices (16 g) bacon, chopped

1 shallot, peeled and finely chopped

1 clove (3 g) peeled garlic, minced or pressed

¼ cup (60 ml) balsamic vinegar

1 teaspoon (5 ml/5 g) mayonnaise

½ cup (125 ml) vegetable oil

¼ cup (60 ml) extra virgin olive oil

Salt and black pepper to taste

1. About 30 minutes before serving, cook the bacon in a skillet over medium heat until it's crispy.

2. Remove the bacon with a slotted spoon and reserve.

3. Reduce the heat to medium-low, add the shallot and cook, stirring frequently, until it's tender and translucent.

4. Add the garlic and continue to cook until it's golden brown and fragrant.

5. Remove the skillet from the heat and reserve the shallot.

6. Put the vinegar and mayonnaise in a blender. With the motor running, add the vegetable oil in a thin, steady stream.

7. Transfer to a bowl and vigorously whisk in the olive oil by hand. (The blender compromises the flavor of extra virgin olive oil.)

8. Stir in the reserved bacon and shallot.

9. Season with salt and pepper.

10. Spoon the vinaigrette over the warm, cooked salmon and serve immediately.

Arctic Char with Thyme Vinaigrette

Makes 4 Servings

This vinaigrette is also great on chicken, cod, duck, halibut, lamb, rabbit, salmon, shellfish, striped bass, and venison. This vinaigrette also makes a great dressing for salad greens.

1½ pounds (0.7 kg) cooked arctic char fillets (see recipe on page 167)

1 tablespoon (15 ml) vegetable oil

1 small onion, peeled and finely chopped, about ½ cup (70 g)

1 jalapeño chile, seeded and chopped, about 1 tablespoon (14 g)

½ cup (125 ml) dry white wine

½ teaspoon (2 ml) dried thyme or 1 teaspoon (5 ml) fresh

¼ teaspoon (1 ml) dried rosemary or ½ teaspoon (2 ml) fresh

2 tablespoons (30 ml) white wine vinegar

1 teaspoon (5 ml) mayonnaise

⅓ cup (80 ml) extra virgin olive oil

Salt and black pepper to taste

1. About 30 minutes before serving, heat the vegetable oil in a skillet over medium heat.

2. Add the onion and jalapeño pepper. Cook, stirring frequently, until the onion is tender and translucent.

3. Add the wine, thyme, and rosemary. Continue cooking until the pan is almost dry. Remove the skillet from the heat and set aside.

4. In a bowl, combine the mayonnaise with the vinegar. Then vigorously whisk in the olive oil in a thin, steady stream.

5. Stir in the onion mixture and season with salt and pepper.

6. Spoon the vinaigrette over the warm, cooked char and serve immediately.

Salmon with Cucumber Dill Sauce

Makes 4 Servings

The sauce in this recipe also goes well on halibut, shrimp, and striped bass.

1½ pounds (0.7 kg) skinless salmon fillets, cut into four
6 ounce (170 g) pieces

2 tablespoons (30 ml/28 g) unsalted butter

½ small onion, peeled and finely chopped, about ¼ cup (35 g)

1 rib celery, trimmed and finely chopped, about ½ cup (40 g)

4 whole cloves

1 bay leaf

Juice of 1 lemon, about 3 tablespoons (45 ml)

Sauce

½ cup (125 ml/130 g) shredded cucumber, peel and seeds removed

¼ cup (60 ml/58 g) sour cream

2 tablespoons (30 ml/29 g) mayonnaise

1 tablespoon (15 ml/8 g) chopped fresh parsley

½ tablespoon (8 ml/2 g) dried dill weed or 1 tablespoon (15 ml) fresh

Salt and black pepper to taste

1. Preheat the water bath to 140°F (60°C) for medium, 122°F (50°C) for medium-rare, or 108°F (42°C) for rare. Immune compromised individuals should never eat rare or medium-rare fish.

2. Meanwhile, melt the butter in a skillet over medium heat.

3. Add the onion and celery. Cook, stirring frequently, until both are tender and the onion is translucent.

4. Add the cloves and bay leaf and continue to cook until fragrant.

5. Transfer the onion mixture to a bowl and stir in the lemon juice. Set aside.

6. Check for and remove any pin-bones from the fillets using needle-nose pliers or tweezers.

7. Divide the onion mixture among four pouches and put a clove and a quarter of the bay leaf into each pouch.

8. Vacuum-seal a piece of salmon in each pouch.

9. Put the sealed pouches into the water bath for 40–50 minutes at 140°F

(60°C) or for 15–20 minutes at 108°F (42°C) or 122°F (50°C).

10. Meanwhile, to make the sauce:

1. In a small bowl, stir together the cucumber, sour cream, mayonnaise, parsley, and dill.
2. Season with salt and pepper.
3. Cover the sauce with plastic wrap and refrigerate until you're ready to serve.

11. Remove the cooked salmon from the pouches and discard the onion mixture.

12. Serve immediately with the chilled sauce.

Salmon with Creamy Olive Sauce
Makes 4 Servings

This sauce also goes well on bass, chicken, cod, duck, grouper, halibut, lamb, pork, rabbit, salmon, and shrimp.

1½ pounds (0.7 kg) salmon fillets, cut into four 6 ounce (170 g) pieces

1 medium onion, peeled and finely chopped, about ¾ cup (110 g)

Juice of 1 lemon, about 3 tablespoons (45 ml)

Sauce

2 tablespoons (30 ml) olive oil

2 cloves (6 g) peeled garlic, minced or pressed

½ cup (125 ml/115 g) cream cheese

Juice of 1 lemon, about 3 tablespoons (45 ml)

1 cup (250 ml/125 g) chopped green olives

¼ teaspoon (1 ml) dried thyme

2 tablespoons (30 ml/8 g) chopped fresh parsley

Salt and black pepper to taste

1. Preheat the water bath to 140°F (60°C) for medium, 122°F (50°C) for medium-rare, or 108°F (42°C) for rare. Immune compromised individuals should never eat rare or medium-rare fish.

2. Put the onion into a microwave safe container and microwave it on high until it's tender and translucent, about 2–3 minutes.

3. Add the lemon juice and divide the onion mixture among four vacuum pouches.

4. Check and remove any pin-bones from the fillets using needle-nose pliers or tweezers.

5. Vacuum-seal a piece of salmon in each pouch with the onions.

6. Put the sealed pouches into the preheated water bath and cook for 40–50 minutes at 140°F (60°C) or for 15–20 minutes at 108°F (42°C) or 122°F (50°C).

7. Meanwhile, to make the sauce:

    1. Heat the oil in a saucepan over medium heat.
    2. Add the garlic and cook until it's golden brown and fragrant.
    3. Add the cream cheese, lemon juice, olives, and thyme. Continue cooking, stirring constantly, until the sauce is smooth.
    4. Reduce the heat to low and stir in the parsley.

5. Season with salt and pepper and cover until you're ready to serve.

8. Remove the salmon from the pouches and discard the onion mixture.

9. Serve immediately, topped with the sauce.

Pan-Seared Scallops

Makes 4 Servings

1½ pounds (0.7 kg) large fresh scallops, preferably diver caught
High-smoke-point oil, such as grapeseed, peanut, or vegetable

1. Preheat the water bath to 140°F (60°C) for medium, 122°F (50°C) for medium-rare, or 108°F (42°C) for rare. Immune compromised individuals should never be served rare or medium-rare shellfish.

2. Vacuum-seal the scallops in several pouches, positioned so that the scallops don't touch each other.

3. Put the sealed pouches into the preheated water bath and cook for 30–40 minutes at 140°F (60°C) or for 15–20 minutes at 108°F (42°C) or 122°F (50°C).

4. Remove the scallops from their pouches and pat them dry with paper towels.

5. Pour just enough oil into a heavy skillet to cover the bottom. Heat the oil over high heat, watching carefully, until it just begins to smoke.

6. Sear the top and bottom of each scallop until it's golden brown, about 15–20 seconds per side. Work in batches, if necessary, to avoid overcrowding the skillet.

7. Serve immediately.

Lobster with Garlic and Lemon Butter Sauce

Makes 4 Servings

Blanching the shelled lobster in boiling water for a few minutes makes removing the meat easier.

4 (5 ounce/150 g) unshelled lobster tails

8 tablespoons (120 ml/110 g) unsalted butter

2 cloves (6 g) peeled garlic, minced or pressed

Juice of 1 lemon, about 3 tablespoons (45 ml)

1. First make the butter sauce by melting the butter in a small pan over medium heat

2. Add the garlic and cook until it's golden brown and fragrant.

3. Remove the pan from the heat and stir in the lemon juice.

4. Let the butter solidify at room temperature until softly solid or refrigerate until needed.

5. When ready to prepare the lobster, preheat the water bath to 140°F (60°C) for medium, 122°F (50°C) for medium-rare, or 108°F (42°C) for rare. Immune compromised individuals should never eat rare or medium rare shellfish.

6. Vacuum-seal the meat of each lobster in a separate pouch with a quarter of the butter mixture.

7. Put the sealed pouches into the preheated water bath and cook for 30–40 minutes at 140°F (60°C) or for 15–20 minutes at 108°F (42°C) or 122°F (50°C).

8. Remove the lobster from the pouches and strain the liquid from the pouch to use as a dipping sauce.

9. Immediately serve the lobster with the sauce on the side.

Shrimp with Garlic

Makes 4 Servings

1½ pounds (0.7 kg) raw peeled shrimp

⅓ cup (80 ml) extra virgin olive oil

2 cloves (6 g) peeled garlic, minced or pressed

1 teaspoon (5 ml) red pepper flakes

1 tablespoon (15 ml) white wine vinegar

1. Preheat the water bath to 140°F (60°C) for medium, 122°F (50°C) for medium-rare, or 108°F (42°C) for rare. Immune compromised individuals should never eat rare or medium-rare shellfish.

2. In a small saucepan over medium heat, combine the olive oil, garlic, red pepper flakes, and vinegar. Cook until the garlic is golden brown and fragrant.

3. Remove from the heat and let the mixture cool slightly.

4. Vacuum-seal the shrimp and the oil mixture in one or more pouches.

5. Put the sealed pouch(es) into the preheated water bath and cook for 30–40 minutes at 140°F (60°C) or for 15–20 minutes at 108°F (42°C) or 122°F (50°C).

6. Remove the shrimp from the pouch and serve immediately.

Shrimp with Peas

Makes 4 Servings

This sauce is also great on beef, chicken, duck, pork, salmon, and scallops.

1½ pounds (0.7 kg) raw peeled shrimp

¼ cup (60 ml) chicken stock

Sauce

1 tablespoon (15 ml) soy sauce

1 tablespoon (15 ml/8 g) cornstarch

1 cup (250 ml) chicken stock

1 teaspoon (5 ml/4 g) granulated sugar

½ cup (120 ml/70 g) frozen peas

1. Preheat the water bath to 140°F (60°C) for medium, 122°F (50°C) for medium-rare, or 108°F (42°C) for rare. Immune compromised individuals should never eat rare or medium-rare shellfish.

2. Put the shrimp and the stock into a heat-stable, resealable pouch, squeeze out the air, and seal. (See discussion page 250.)

3. Put the sealed pouch(es) into the preheated water bath and cook for 30–40 minutes at 140°F (60°C) or for 15–20 minutes at 108°F (42°C) or 122°F (50°C).

4. About 20 minutes before serving, make a slurry by stirring the cornstarch into the soy sauce.

5. Combine the soy sauce slurry, stock, and sugar in a saucepan over medium heat. Cook, stirring constantly, until the sauce has cleared and thickened.

6. Stir in the frozen peas and continue cooking until they're tender.

7. Remove the shrimp from the pouch(es) and toss them with the sauce. Serve immediately.

Vegetables, Fruits & Legumes

While vegetables are a rich source of vitamins and minerals, boiled or steamed vegetables lose nutrients to their cooking water. Sous vide cooked vegetables, in comparison, retain nearly all their nutritive value. This superior retention of nutrients also intensifies the flavor inherent in the vegetable and can cause some vegetables, such as turnips and rutabaga, to have a flavor that's too pronounced for some palates.

Vegetables that are boiled, steamed, or microwaved lose their nutrients because the cell walls are damaged by the heat and allow the water and nutrients in the cells to leach out. Sous vide vegetables leave the cell walls mostly intact and make the vegetables tender by dissolving some of the cementing material that holds the cells together. In vegetables, this cementing material starts to dissolve around 180–185°F (82–85°C). Starchy vegetables can be cooked at the slightly lower temperature of 175°F (80°C) because their texture is also changed by the gelatinization of the starch granules in their cells.

Though fruits are often eaten raw, it's sometimes nice to cook apples and pears until they're tender. Tart (high acid) apples, such as Granny Smith, soften faster than sweet (low acid) apples, such as Gala or Fuji, because the acid lowers the temperature at which the cementing material dissolves.

Legumes (beans, peas, lentils) are cooked to gelatinize their starches, make their proteins more digestible, and to weaken the cementing material that holds their cells together so you can chew them. Legumes cooked sous vide don't need to be soaked, because they can absorb the same amount of water in 50 minutes at 195°F (90°C) as they would in 16 hours at room temperature. Moreover, since the legumes are cooked in their soaking water, their water-soluble vitamins and minerals are retained.

Since vegetables, fruits, and legumes are cooked in 175–195°F (80–90°C) water baths, their pouches may balloon and need to be held under the surface of the water with a metal rack. The pouches balloon because the residual air left in the pouch after vacuum sealing expands and because some of the moisture in the food is converted into water vapor.

Asparagus
Makes 4 Servings

8 ounces (225 g) green or white asparagus

2 tablespoons (30 ml/28 g) unsalted butter

Zest of 1 lemon, about 1 tablespoon (15 ml)

Salt and black pepper

1. Preheat the water bath to 185°F (85°C).

2. Snap off the woody stem of each piece of asparagus.

3. Thoroughly wash the asparagus by first soaking them in cold water and then rinsing them under cold running water.

4. Vacuum-seal the asparagus, butter, and lemon zest in a large pouch so that they're in a single layer.

5. Put the sealed pouch into the preheated water bath and cook them for 45–60 minutes.

6. Remove the asparagus from the pouch, season with salt and pepper, and serve immediately.

Green Beans

Makes 4 Servings

8 ounces (225 g) fresh green beans

¼ small onion, peeled and finely chopped

2 tablespoons (30 ml/28 g) unsalted butter

1 slice (8 g) bacon, cooked

Salt and black pepper

1. Preheat the water bath to 185°F (85°C).

2. Thoroughly wash and trim the green beans to remove the stems and strings.

3. To keep the green beans a brighter green, blanch them in boiling water and then shock them in ice water before cooking them sous vide.

    1. Bring a large pot of water to a vigorous boil.
    2. Drop the beans into the water and cook them for only 10–15 seconds.
    3. Remove the beans from the boiling water and immediately put them into a bowl of ice cold water.

4. Vacuum-seal the green beans, onion, butter, bacon, and a pinch of salt and pepper in a large pouch.

5. Put the sealed pouch into the preheated water bath and cook for 45–60 minutes.

6. Remove the green beans from the pouch and serve immediately.

Beets

Makes 4 Servings

4 young beets, about 3 inches (8 cm) in diameter

¼ cup (60 ml) cider vinegar

¼ cup (60 ml/50 g) granulated sugar

2 tablespoons (30 ml/28 g) unsalted butter

1 pinch salt

1. Preheat the water bath to 185°F (85°C).

2. Scrub the beets thoroughly under running water. Trim the root ends, peel, and cut into ½ inch (1 cm) slices.

3. While the water bath comes up to temperature, vacuum-seal the beets, vinegar, sugar, butter, and salt in a large pouch, so that the slices don't overlap.

4. Put the sealed pouch into the preheated water bath and cook for 1½–2 hours.

5. Remove the beets from the pouch.

6. Pour the liquid from the pouch into a small saucepan and reduce the liquid until it is thick enough to coat the back of a spoon.

7. Serve the beets topped with the sauce.

Broccoli

Makes 4 Servings

2 bunches broccoli
2 tablespoons (30 ml/28 g) unsalted butter
Salt and black pepper

1. Preheat the water bath to 185°F (85°C).

2. Trim the broccoli into florets and thoroughly wash them.

3. To keep the broccoli a brighter green, blanch the florets in boiling water and then shock them in ice water before cooking them sous vide.

   1. Bring a large pot of water to a vigorous boil.
   2. Drop the florets into the water and cook them for only 10–15 seconds.
   3. Remove the florets from the boiling water and immediately put them into a bowl of ice cold water.

4. Vacuum-seal the broccoli, butter, and a pinch of salt and pepper in a large pouch so that the florets are in a single layer.

5. Put the sealed pouch into the preheated water bath and cook for 25–35 minutes.

6. Remove the broccoli from the pouch and serve immediately.

Brussels Sprouts
Makes 4 Servings

For a little variation, add 1 slice of cooked and chopped bacon to the pouch before vacuum-sealing.

8 ounces (225 g) brussels sprouts
2 tablespoons (30 ml/28 g) unsalted butter
Salt and black pepper

1. Preheat the water bath to 185°F (85°C).

2. Thoroughly wash the sprouts by soaking them in cold water and then rinsing them under cold running water.

3. Trim the ends and remove any discolored leaves.

4. Vacuum-seal the sprouts, butter, and a pinch of salt and pepper in a large pouch so that they're in a single layer.

5. Put the sealed pouch into the preheated water bath and cook for 45–60 minutes.

6. Remove the sprouts from the pouch and serve immediately.

Cabbage
Makes 4 Servings

1 small head red or green cabbage, about 4 ½ inches (11 cm) in diameter
2 tablespoons (30 ml/28 g) unsalted butter
Salt and black pepper

1. Preheat the water bath to 185°F (85°C).

2. Remove any wilted outside leaves and shred the head.

3. Soak the shredded cabbage in cold water, and then rinse under cold running water and drain. (You can also use a package of pre-washed, shredded cabbage.)

4. Vacuum-seal the cabbage, butter, and a pinch of salt and pepper in a large pouch.

5. Put the sealed pouch into the preheated water bath and cook for 30–45 minutes.

6. Remove the cabbage from the pouch and serve immediately.

Carrots

Makes 4 Servings

8 ounces (225 g) carrots
2 tablespoons (30 ml/28 g) unsalted butter
1 tablespoon (15 ml/21 g) honey
¼ teaspoon (1 ml) sage
Salt and black pepper

1. Preheat the water bath to 185°F (85°C).
2. While the water bath comes up to temperature, thoroughly wash, peel, and slice the carrots. (You can also use pre-washed baby carrots.)
3. Vacuum-seal the carrots, butter, honey, sage, and a pinch of salt and pepper in a large pouch so that they're in a single layer.
4. Put the sealed pouch into the preheated water bath and cook for 30–50 minutes.
5. Remove the carrots from the pouch and serve immediately.

Cauliflower

Makes 4 Servings

1 head cauliflower
2 tablespoons (30 ml/28 g) unsalted butter
¼ teaspoon (1 ml) red pepper flakes (optional)
Salt and black pepper

1. Preheat the water bath to 185°F (85°C).
2. Trim the stem and break the cauliflower into florets.
3. Thoroughly wash the florets by soaking them in cold water and then rinsing them under cold running water.
4. While the water bath comes up to temperature, vacuum-seal the cauliflower, butter, red pepper flakes, and a pinch of salt and pepper in a large pouch so that the florets are in a single layer.
5. Put the sealed pouch into the preheated water bath and cook for 25–35 minutes.
6. Remove the cauliflower from the pouch and serve immediately.

Celery Root (Celeriac)
Makes 4 Servings

1 celery root (celeriac)
2 tablespoons (30 ml/28 g) unsalted butter
¼ teaspoon (1 ml) dried ground tarragon
Salt and black pepper

1. Preheat the water bath to 185°F (85°C).

2. Cut off any leaves and wash thoroughly. Trim the root and stalk ends of the celery root and cut off the thick skin. Cut the celery root into ¼ inch (50–60 mm) slices. Cut the slices in half or in quarters to make bite-size pieces.

3. Vacuum-seal the celery root slices in a single layer with the butter, tarragon, and a pinch of salt and pepper.

4. Put the sealed pouch into the preheated water bath and cook for 1–1½ hours.

5. Remove the celery root from the pouch and serve immediately.

Corn
Makes 4 Servings

4 ears corn, cleaned (husks and silk removed, if present)
4 tablespoons (60 ml/65 g) unsalted butter
Salt and black pepper to taste

1. Preheat the water bath to 185°F (85°C).

2. Vacuum-seal the corn and butter in two large pouches.

3. Put the sealed pouches into the preheated water bath and cook for 30–45 minutes.

4. Remove the corn from the pouches, season with salt and pepper, and serve immediately.

Leeks

Makes 4 Servings

2 medium leeks
2 tablespoons (30 ml/28 g) unsalted butter
Salt and black pepper

1. Preheat the water bath to 185°F (85°C).

2. Cut off all but about 2 inches (5 cm) of the green tops and trim the root ends of the leeks.

3. Thoroughly wash the leeks under cold running water.

4. Vacuum-seal the leeks, butter, and a pinch of salt and pepper in a large pouch.

5. Put the sealed pouch into the preheated water bath and cook for 45–60 minutes.

6. Remove the leeks from the pouch, slice into bite-size pieces, and serve immediately.

Onions

Makes 4 Servings

Onions cooked sous vide have a surprisingly mild flavor.

2 medium onions
2 tablespoons (30 ml/28 g) unsalted butter

1. Preheat the water bath to 185°F (85°C).

2. Trim the root and stem ends of the onion and peel away the skin and the outermost layer.

3. Vacuum-seal the onions and butter in a large pouch.

4. Put the sealed pouch in the preheated water bath and cook for 1–1½ hours.

5. Remove the onions from the pouch, slice into bite-size pieces, and serve immediately.

Parsnips

Makes 4 Servings

2 medium parsnips
2 tablespoons (30 ml/28 g) unsalted butter
Salt and black pepper
Cinnamon and sugar to taste

1. Preheat the water bath to 185°F (85°C).

2. Thoroughly scrub the parsnips under cold running water.

3. Peel the parsnips and cut them into ¼ inch (50–60 mm) slices. Cut the larger slices in half to make them bite-size.

4. Vacuum-seal them in a pouch with the butter and a pinch of salt and pepper so that they're in a single layer

5. Put the sealed pouch into the preheated water bath and cook for 30–45 minutes.

6. Remove the parsnips from the pouch, sprinkle with cinnamon and sugar, and serve immediately.

Fresh Peas

Makes 4 Servings

8 ounces (225 g) fresh green peas
2 tablespoons (30 ml/28 g) unsalted butter
Salt and black pepper

1. Preheat the water bath to 175°F (80°C).

2. Shell the peas and then wash them thoroughly.

3. Vacuum-seal the peas, butter, and a pinch of salt and pepper in a large pouch.

4. Put the sealed pouch into the preheated water bath and cook for 30–40 minutes.

5. Remove the peas from the pouch and serve immediately.

  Variation: Substitute frozen peas for the fresh peas and add 5–10 minutes to the cooking time.

Potatoes

Makes 4 Servings

4 medium potatoes
¼ teaspoon (1 ml) garlic powder (optional)
Salt and black pepper
2 tablespoons (30 ml/28 g) unsalted butter

1. Preheat the water bath to 175°F (80°C).
2. Scrub the potatoes under cold running water.
3. Remove the eyes and, if desired, peel the potatoes.
4. Cut the potatoes into bite-size pieces.
5. Season the potatoes with the garlic powder and a pinch of salt and pepper.
6. Vacuum-seal the potatoes and butter in a large pouch so that they're in a single layer.
7. Put the sealed pouch into the preheated water bath and cook for 1–1½ hours.
8. Remove the potatoes from the pouch and serve immediately.

Sweet Potatoes

Makes 4 Servings

2 medium sweet potatoes or yams
1 tablespoon (15 ml/14 g) brown sugar
2 tablespoons (30 ml/28 g) unsalted butter

1. Preheat the water bath to 175°F (80°C).
2. Thoroughly wash and peel the sweet potatoes, and cut them into bite-size pieces.
3. Sprinkle the sugar over the pieces and vacuum-seal them in a large pouch with the butter.
4. Put the sealed pouch into the preheated water bath and cook for 1–1¼ hours.
5. Remove the sweet potato pieces from the pouch and serve immediately.

Pumpkin

Makes 4 Servings

1 small pumpkin
2 tablespoons (30 ml/28 g) unsalted butter
Salt and black pepper

1. Preheat the water bath to 175°F (80°C).

2. Wash the pumpkin and cut it into pieces.

3. Peel the pieces and remove the seeds. (You may either discard the seeds or sprinkle them with salt and toast them on a cookie sheet in a 350°F (175°C) oven until they're lightly browned.)

4. Cut the slices of pumpkin into bite-size pieces. Vacuum-seal the pieces in a large pouch with the butter and a pinch of salt and pepper, so that they're in a single layer

5. Put the sealed pouch into the preheated water bath and cook for 1–1½ hours.

6. Remove the pumpkin from the pouch and serve immediately.

Rutabagas

Makes 4 Servings

Rutabagas cooked sous vide have a very pronounced flavor that may be too much for people who don't love rutabagas, but will delight those who do.

2 medium rutabagas or yellow turnips
2 tablespoons (30 ml/28 g) unsalted butter
¼ teaspoon (1 ml) dried thyme
Salt and black pepper

1. Preheat the water bath to 185°F (85°C).

2. Wash and peel the rutabagas. Cut the rutabagas into bite-size pieces.

3. Vacuum-seal the rutabagas, butter, thyme, and a pinch of salt and pepper in a large pouch so that they're in a single layer.

4. Put the sealed pouches into the preheated water bath and cook for 2–2½ hours.

5. Remove the rutabagas from the pouch and serve immediately.

Acorn Squash
Makes 4 Servings

2 medium acorn squash
4 tablespoons (60 ml/56 g) unsalted butter
¼ cup (60 ml/55 g) brown sugar

1. Preheat the water bath to 175°F (80°C).
2. Thoroughly wash the surface of the squash.
3. Cut the squash in half and scrape out the stringy center portion with a spoon.
4. Divide the butter and brown sugar among the four squash halves.
5. Vacuum-seal each piece of squash in a separate pouch.
6. Put the sealed pouches into the preheated water bath and cook for 2–2 ¼ hours.
7. Remove the squash from the pouches and serve immediately.

Butternut Squash
Makes 4 Servings

1 large butternut squash
4 tablespoons (60 ml/56 g) unsalted butter
Cinnamon and sugar to taste

1. Preheat the water bath to 175°F (80°C).
2. Thoroughly wash the surface of the squash, trim off the ends, and peel.
3. Carefully slice in half lengthwise and scrape out the stringy portion.
4. Cut the squash into bite-size pieces.
5. Vacuum-seal the pieces of squash with the butter in one or more pouches, so that they're in a single layer.
6. Put the sealed pouch(es) into the preheated water bath and cook for 2–2 ¼ hours.
7. Remove the squash from the pouch(es) and serve immediately.

Summer Squash

Makes 4 Servings

**1 large summer squash, such as yellow crookneck or straightneck;
or 2 scallop or patty pan squash**

2 tablespoons (30 ml) extra virgin olive oil

¼ teaspoon (1 ml) red pepper flakes

Salt and black pepper

1. Preheat the water bath to 185°F (85°C).

2. Wash the squash and cut it into bite-size pieces.

3. Toss the squash, olive oil, red pepper flakes, and a pinch of salt and pepper in a bowl.

4. Vacuum-seal the squash in one or more large pouches, so that they're in a single layer.

5. Put the sealed pouches into the preheated water bath and cook for 45–60 minutes.

6. Remove the squash from the pouches and serve immediately.

Turnips

Makes 4 Servings

Sous vide cooking brings out the inherent flavor of foods, and turnips cooked sous vide may have too pronounced a turnip flavor for people who don't love turnips.

2 medium white turnips

2 tablespoons (30 ml/28 g) unsalted butter

Salt and black pepper

1. Preheat the water bath to 185°F (85°C).

2. Wash and peel the turnips, and cut them into bite-size pieces.

3. Vacuum-seal the turnips, butter, and a pinch of salt and pepper in a large pouch, so that they're in a single layer.

4. Put the sealed pouches into the preheated water bath and cook for 30–60 minutes.

5. Remove the turnips from the pouches and serve immediately.

Zucchini

Makes 4 Servings

1 large zucchini
2 tablespoons (30 ml) extra virgin olive oil
Salt and black pepper

1. Preheat the water bath to 185°F (85°C).

2. Wash the zucchini and cut it into bite-size pieces.

3. Toss the zucchini with olive oil and a pinch of salt and pepper in a bowl to coat.

4. Vacuum-seal the zucchini in a single layer in a large pouch.

5. Put the sealed pouch into the preheated water bath and cook for 30–45 minutes.

6. Remove the zucchini from the pouch and serve immediately.

Apples

Makes 4 Servings

4 medium apples, peeled and sliced
2 tablespoons (30 ml/28 g) unsalted butter
1 tablespoon (15 ml/14 g) brown sugar
¼ teaspoon (1 ml) ground cinnamon

1. Preheat the water bath to 185°F (85°C).

2. Put the sliced apples, butter, sugar, and cinnamon into a large pouch. Hold the top of the pouch closed and shake vigorously to evenly distribute the sugar and cinnamon.

3. Vacuum-seal the pouch so that the apples are in a single layer.

4. Put the sealed pouch into the preheated water bath and cook for 30–40 minutes.

5. Remove the apples from the pouch and serve immediately.

Pears

Makes 4 Servings

4 medium pears, sliced

1. Preheat the water bath to 185°F (85°C).

2. Vacuum-seal the sliced pears in a large pouch, so that they're in a single layer.

3. Put the sealed pouch into the preheated water bath and cook for 25–35 minutes.

4. Remove the pears from the pouch and serve immediately.

Dried Beans

Makes 4 Servings

The cooking time of beans depends on the age of beans, when in the season they were harvested, and the hardness of the water. So if the beans aren't tender enough after cooking sous vide, transfer them to a saucepan, and simmer them over medium heat until they're tender.

1 cup (8 ounces/250 ml/225 g) dried lentils or black, cranberry, garbanzo (chickpeas), great northern, kidney, navy (Yankee), or pinto beans

3 cups (750 ml) water

Aromatics or herbs, such as a chopped onions, minced garlic cloves, a chile pepper, fresh herbs, or a bay leaf

1 teaspoon (5 ml) table salt

1. Preheat the water bath 195°F (90°C).

2. Rinse the dried beans under running water.

3. Discard any damaged beans, dirt, or stones.

4. Put the rinsed beans, water, and any aromatics or herbs, if using, in a large, heat-stable, resealable pouch. Squeeze out as much air as possible and seal.

5. Put the sealed pouch of beans into the water bath and cook: ¾−1 hour for lentils; 2½−3½ hours for cranberry, navy or Yankee beans; 3−4 hours for great northern or kidney beans; 3½−4½ hours for black beans, 4−5 hours for pinto beans; or 5−6 hours for chickpeas or garbanzo beans.

6. Remove the pouch from the water bath.

7. Pour the beans and cooking liquid into a large bowl and stir in the salt.

8. Strain the cooked beans and serve.

Desserts

French or custard ice cream bases are incredibly easy to make sous vide. French style ice cream is made from a stirred custard known as a crème anglaise. The traditional method of making crème anglaise is a time-consuming and labor-intensive process that requires: scalding the milk and cream; whisking the egg yolks into the sugar until lightened in color; tempering a third of the hot milk mixture into the yolk mixture while whisking constantly; adding the tempered yolk mixture to the pan; cooking slowly, while whisking constantly, until the custard just thickens but before it curdles; and straining it into a bowl over ice water and stirring until it's cold. The hands-on time for making sous vide crème anglaise is trivial in comparison. Simply put all the cold ingredients into a blender and process it until it's smooth; seal the mixture in a pouch; put the pouch into your water bath for 20 minutes; and drop the sealed pouch into ice water until it's cold. It really couldn't be easier.

Vanilla Ice Cream
Makes 8 Servings

2 cups (500 ml) whole milk

1 cup (240 ml) heavy cream

6 large (100 g) egg yolks

Seeds of 2 vanilla pods

½ cup (60 g) nonfat dry milk powder

½ cup (100 g) granulated sugar

1 pinch salt

1. Preheat the water bath to 181°F (82°C).

2. Remove the seeds from the vanilla pods by slicing them lengthwise and scraping the seeds out with the tip of a paring knife.

3. Combine the vanilla seeds, milk, cream, egg yolks, milk powder, sugar, and salt in a blender or food processor and process until smooth.

4. Pour the ice cream base into a large, heat-stable, resealable pouch, squeeze out all the air, and seal.

5. Put the sealed pouch into the water bath and cook for about 20 minutes.

6. Transfer the sealed pouch to an ice water bath that's at least half ice for about 20 minutes. Agitate the pouch two or three times during the chilling period. (If you have the time, refrigerate the ice cream base for 8–24 hours to allow the flavors to meld and the fat to crystallize, which will give the finished ice cream a smoother texture.)

7. When ready to churn, pour the chilled ice cream base into an ice cream maker and churn it according to the manufacturer's instructions. The churned ice cream should have the consistency of soft-serve ice cream (and reach about 23°F/−5°C).

8. Transfer the ice cream to a container, press plastic wrap to the surface, and put it into a freezer to harden for about an hour.

Chocolate Ice Cream
Makes 8 Servings

2 cups (500 g) whole milk

1 cup (250 g) heavy cream

6 large (100 g) egg yolks

½ cup (40 g) unsweetened cocoa powder

½ cup (100 g) granulated sugar

½ cup (60 g) nonfat dry milk powder

1 teaspoon (5 ml) instant espresso powder

1 pinch salt

1. Preheat the water bath to 181°F (82°C).

2. Combine the milk, cream, egg yolks, cocoa powder, sugar, milk powder, espresso powder, and salt in a blender or food processor and process until smooth.

3. Pour the ice cream base into a large, heat-stable, resealable pouch, squeeze out all the air, and seal.

4. Put the sealed pouch into the water bath and cook for about 20 minutes.

5. Transfer the sealed pouch to an ice water bath that's at least half ice for about 20 minutes. Agitate the pouch two or three times during the chilling period. (If you have the time, refrigerate the ice cream base for 8–24 hours to allow the flavors to meld and the fat to crystallize, which will give the finished ice cream a smoother texture.)

6. When ready to churn, pour the chilled ice cream base into an ice cream maker and churn it according to the manufacturer's instructions. The churned ice cream should have the consistency of soft-serve ice cream (and reach about 23°F/−5°C).

7. Transfer the ice cream to a container, press plastic wrap to the surface, and put it into a freezer to harden for about an hour.

> *Variation: To make Chocolate Gelato, use 3 cups (720 g) whole milk and no cream, increase the sugar to ⅔ cup (130 g), and decrease the milk powder to ⅓ cup (40 g).*

Strawberry Ice Cream
Makes 8 Servings

12 ounces (350 g) cored and diced fresh (or thawed frozen) strawberries

1 cup (240 g) heavy cream

½ cup (120 g) whole milk

6 large (100 g) egg yolks

¾ cup (90 g) nonfat dry milk powder

½ cup (100 g) granulated sugar

1 pinch salt

1. Preheat the water bath to 181°F (82°C).

2. Combine strawberries, cream, milk, egg yolks, milk powder, sugar, and salt in a blender or food processor and process until smooth.

3. Pour the ice cream base into a large, heat-stable, resealable pouch, squeeze out all the air, and seal.

4. Put the sealed pouch into the water bath and cook for about 20 minutes.

5. Transfer the sealed pouch to an ice water bath that's at least half ice for about 20 minutes. Agitate the pouch two or three times during the chilling period. (If you have the time, refrigerate the ice cream base for 8 24 hours to allow the flavors to meld and the fat to crystallize, which will give the finished ice cream a smoother texture.)

6. When ready to churn, pour the chilled ice cream base into an ice cream maker and churn it according to the manufacturer's instructions. The churned ice cream should have the consistency of soft-serve ice cream (and reach about 23°F/−5°C).

7. Transfer the ice cream to a container, press plastic wrap to the surface, and put it into a freezer to harden for about an hour.

Variation: To make Strawberry Gelato, use 1½ cups (350 g) whole milk and no cream, decrease the milk powder to ½ cup (60 g), and increase the sugar to ¾ cup (150 g).

Peach Ice Cream
Makes 8 Servings

4 ripe medium peaches, peeled and diced, about 21 ounces (600 g)

1 cup (240 g) heavy cream

6 large (100 g) egg yolks

1 cup (120 g) nonfat dry milk powder

⅓ cup (70 g) granulated sugar

1 pinch salt

1. Preheat the water bath to 181°F (82°C).

2. Combine the peaches, cream, egg yolks, milk powder, sugar, and salt in a blender or food processor and process until smooth.

3. Pour the ice cream base into a large, heat-stable, resealable pouch, squeeze out all the air, and seal.

4. Put the sealed pouch into the water bath and cook for about 20 minutes.

5. Transfer the sealed pouch to an ice water bath that's at least half ice for about 20 minutes. Agitate the pouch two or three times during the chilling period. (If you have the time, refrigerate the ice cream base for 8–24 hours to allow the flavors to meld and the fat to crystallize, which will give the finished ice cream a smoother texture.)

6. When ready to churn, pour the chilled ice cream base into an ice cream maker and churn it according to the manufacturer's instructions. The churned ice cream should have the consistency of soft-serve ice cream (and reach about 23°F/−5°C).

7. Transfer the ice cream to a container, press plastic wrap to the surface, and put it into a freezer to harden for about an hour.

Variation: For Peach Gelato, use only 3 medium ripe peaches, use 1 cup (245 g) whole milk instead of the cream, decrease the milk powder to ¾ cup (90 g), and double the sugar to ⅔ cup (130 g).

Mint Gelato

Makes 8 Servings

3 cups (750 ml) whole milk

½ cup (13 g) fresh spearmint leaves

6 large (300 g) large eggs

½ cup (60 g) nonfat dry milk powder

1 cup (200 g) granulated sugar

1 pinch salt

1. Put the mint leaves into the milk, cover and refrigerate overnight to infuse the milk with mint.

2. Preheat the water bath to 181°F (82°C).

3. Strain the milk into a blender or food processor and discard the mint leaves. Add the eggs, milk powder, sugar, and salt. Process until smooth.

4. Pour the gelato base into a large, heat-stable, resealable pouch, squeeze out all the air, and seal.

5. Put the sealed pouch into the water bath and cook for about 20 minutes.

6. Transfer the sealed pouch to an ice water bath that's at least half ice for about 20 minutes. Agitate the pouch two or three times during the chilling period. (If you have the time, refrigerate the gelato base for 8–24 hours to allow the flavors to meld and the fat to crystallize, which will give the finished gelato a smoother texture.)

7. When ready to churn, pour the chilled gelato base into an gelato maker and churn it according to the manufacturer's instructions. The churned gelato should have the consistency of soft-serve gelato (and reach about 23°F/–5°C).

8. Transfer the gelato to a container, press plastic wrap to the surface, and put it into a freezer to harden for about an hour.

Variation: After churning the gelato, stir in 1 cup (8 ounces/ 250 ml/170 g) semi-sweet chocolate chips.

Fresh Apple Ice Cream
Makes 8 Servings

This is great topped with the caramel sauce on page 245.

2 large tart apples, peeled and diced, about 15 ounces (425 g)

1 cup (240 g) heavy cream

⅓ cup (70 g) granulated sugar

6 large (100 g) egg yolks

¾ cup (90 g) nonfat dry milk powder

Juice of 1 lemon, about 3 tablespoons (45 ml)

1 pinch salt

1. Preheat the water bath to 181°F (82°C).

2. Combine apples, cream, sugar, egg yolks, milk powder, lemon juice, and salt in a blender or food processor and process until smooth.

3. Pour the ice cream base into a large, heat-stable, resealable pouch, squeeze out all the air, and seal.

4. Put the sealed pouch into the water bath and cook for about 20 minutes.

5. Transfer the sealed pouch to an ice water bath that's at least half ice for about 20 minutes. Agitate the pouch two or three times during the chilling period. (If you have the time, refrigerate the ice cream base for 8–24 hours to allow the flavors to meld and the fat to crystallize, which will give the finished ice cream a smoother texture.)

6. When ready to churn, pour the chilled ice cream base into an ice cream maker and churn it according to the manufacturer's instructions. The churned ice cream should have the consistency of soft-serve ice cream (and reach about 23°F/–5°C).

7. Transfer the ice cream to a container, press plastic wrap to the surface, and put it into a freezer to harden for about an hour.

Variation: For Fresh Apple Gelato, use 1 cup (245 g) whole milk instead of cream and increase the sugar to ½ cup (100 g).

Banana Ice Cream

Makes 8 Servings

This is especially good topped with the chocolate sauce on page 245.

2 large very ripe bananas, about 10 ounces (270 g)

1 cup (240 ml) heavy cream

1 cup (240 ml) whole milk

6 large (100 g) egg yolks

¾ cup (90 g) nonfat dry milk powder

⅓ cup (70 g) granulated sugar

1 pinch salt

1. Preheat the water bath to 181°F (82°C).

2. Combine the bananas, cream, milk, egg yolks, milk powder, sugar, and salt in a blender or food processor and process until smooth.

3. Pour the ice cream base into a large, heat-stable, resealable pouch, squeeze out all the air, and seal.

4. Put the sealed pouch into the water bath and cook for about 20 minutes.

5. Transfer the sealed pouch to an ice water bath that's at least half ice for about 20 minutes. Agitate the pouch two or three times during the chilling period. (If you have the time, refrigerate the ice cream base for 8–24 hours to allow the flavors to meld and the fat to crystallize, which will give the finished ice cream a smoother texture.)

6. When ready to churn, pour the chilled ice cream base into an ice cream maker and churn it according to the manufacturer's instructions. The churned ice cream should have the consistency of soft-serve ice cream (and reach about 23°F/−5°C).

7. Transfer the ice cream to a container, press plastic wrap to the surface, and put it into a freezer to harden for about an hour.

Variation: For Banana Gelato, use 3 large bananas, increase the whole milk to 1½ cups (360 ml) and no cream, decrease the milk powder to ½ cup (60 g), and increase the sugar to ½ cup (100 g).

Coffee Ice Cream
Makes 8 Servings

2 cups (500 ml) whole milk

1 cup (250 ml) heavy cream

6 large (100 g) egg yolks

½ c (100 g) granulated sugar

¼ c (12 g) instant regular coffee powder

½ c (60 g) nonfat dry milk powder

1 pinch salt

1. Preheat the water bath to 181°F (82°C).

2. Combine the milk, cream, egg yolks, sugar, coffee powder, milk powder, and salt in a blender or food processor and process until smooth.

3. Pour the ice cream base into a large, heat-stable, resealable pouch, squeeze out all the air, and seal.

4. Put the sealed pouch into the water bath and cook for about 20 minutes.

5. Transfer the sealed pouch to an ice water bath that's at least half ice for about 20 minutes. Agitate the pouch two or three times during the chilling period. (If you have the time, refrigerate the ice cream base for 8–24 hours to allow the flavors to meld and the fat to crystallize, which will give the finished ice cream a smoother texture.)

6. When ready to churn, pour the chilled ice cream base into an ice cream maker and churn it according to the manufacturer's instructions. The churned ice cream should have the consistency of soft-serve ice cream (and reach about 23°F/−5°C).

7. Transfer the ice cream to a container, press plastic wrap to the surface, and put it into a freezer to harden for about an hour.

Variation: For Coffee Gelato, use 3 cups (750 g) whole milk and no cream, increase the sugar to 1 cup (200 g), and decrease the milk powder to ¼ cup (30 g).

Peanut Butter Ice Cream
Makes 8 Servings

This recipe is amazing topped with the chocolate sauce on page 245.

2½ cups (600 ml) whole milk

½ cup (125 ml/125 g) smooth peanut butter

6 large (100 g) egg yolks

½ cup (60 g) nonfat dry milk powder

½ cup (100 g) granulated sugar

1. Preheat the water bath to 181°F (82°C).

2. Combine the milk, peanut butter, egg yolks, milk powder, and sugar in a blender or food processor and process until smooth.

3. Pour the ice cream base into a large, heat-stable, resealable pouch, squeeze out all the air, and seal.

4. Put the sealed pouch into the water bath and cook for about 20 minutes.

5. Transfer the sealed pouch to an ice water bath that's at least half ice for about 20 minutes. Agitate the pouch two or three times during the chilling period. (If you have the time, refrigerate the ice cream base for 8–24 hours to allow the flavors to meld and the fat to crystallize, which will give the finished ice cream a smoother texture.)

6. When ready to churn, pour the chilled ice cream base into an ice cream maker and churn it according to the manufacturer's instructions. The churned ice cream should have the consistency of soft-serve ice cream (and reach about 23°F/−5°C).

7. Transfer the ice cream to a container, press plastic wrap to the surface, and put it into a freezer to harden for about an hour.

Nutella Gelato
Makes 8 Servings

3 cups (720 ml) whole milk

⅓ cup (100 g) Nutella® or other chocolate-flavored hazelnut spread

6 large (100 g) egg yolks

⅓ cup (40 g) nonfat dry milk powder

⅓ cup (70 g) granulated sugar

1. Preheat the water bath to 181°F (82°C).

2. Combine the milk, Nutella,® egg yolks, milk powder, and sugar in a blender or food processor and process until smooth.

3. Pour the gelato base into a large, heat-stable, resealable pouch, squeeze out all the air, and seal.

4. Put the sealed pouch into the water bath and cook for about 20 minutes.

5. Transfer the sealed pouch to an ice water bath that's at least half ice for about 20 minutes. Agitate the pouch two or three times during the chilling period. (If you have the time, refrigerate the gelato base for 8–24 hours to allow the flavors to meld and the fat to crystallize, which will give the finished gelato a smoother texture.)

6. When ready to churn, pour the chilled gelato base into an gelato maker and churn it according to the manufacturer's instructions. The churned gelato should have the consistency of soft-serve gelato (and reach about 23°F/−5°C).

7. Transfer the gelato to a container, press plastic wrap to the surface, and put it into a freezer to harden for about an hour.

Cinnamon Ice Cream
Makes 8 Servings

2 cups (500 ml) whole milk

1 cup (250 ml) heavy cream

6 large (100 g) egg yolks

½ cup (100 g) granulated sugar

½ cup (60 g) nonfat dry milk powder

2 tablespoon (30 ml/15 g) ground cinnamon

1 pinch salt

1. Preheat the water bath to 181°F (82°C).

2. Combine the milk, cream, egg yolks, sugar, milk powder, cinnamon, and salt in a blender or food processor and process until smooth.

3. Pour the ice cream base into a large, heat-stable, resealable pouch, squeeze out all the air, and seal.

4. Put the sealed pouch into the water bath and cook for about 20 minutes.

5. Transfer the sealed pouch to an ice water bath that's at least half ice for about 20 minutes. Agitate the pouch two or three times during the chilling period. (If you have the time, refrigerate the ice cream base for 8–24 hours to allow the flavors to meld and the fat to crystallize, which will give the finished ice cream a smoother texture.)

6. When ready to churn, pour the chilled ice cream base into an ice cream maker and churn it according to the manufacturer's instructions. The churned ice cream should have the consistency of soft-serve ice cream (and reach about 23°F/–5°C).

7. Transfer the ice cream to a container, press plastic wrap to the surface, and put it into a freezer to harden for about an hour.

> *Variation: To make Cinnamon Gelato, use 3 cups (720 ml) whole milk and no cream, increase the sugar to ¾ cup (150 g), and decrease the milk powder to ⅓ cup (40 g).*

Coconut Ice Cream
Makes 8 Servings

1½ cups (360 ml) whole milk

1½ cups (360 ml) canned coconut milk

6 large (100 g) egg yolks

¾ cup (90 g) nonfat dry milk powder

½ cup (100 g) granulated sugar

1. Preheat the water bath to 181°F (82°C).

2. Combine the whole milk, coconut milk, egg yolks, milk powder, and sugar in a blender or food processor and process until smooth.

3. Pour the ice cream base into a large, heat-stable, resealable pouch, squeeze out all the air, and seal.

4. Put the sealed pouch into the water bath and cook for about 20 minutes.

5. Transfer the sealed pouch to an ice water bath that's at least half ice for about 20 minutes. Agitate the pouch two or three times during the chilling period. (If you have the time, refrigerate the ice cream base for 8–24 hours to allow the flavors to meld and the fat to crystallize, which will give the finished ice cream a smoother texture.)

6. When ready to churn, pour the chilled ice cream base into an ice cream maker and churn it according to the manufacturer's instructions. The churned ice cream should have the consistency of soft-serve ice cream (and reach about 23°F/−5°C).

7. Transfer the ice cream to a container, press plastic wrap to the surface, and put it into a freezer to harden for about an hour.

Chocolate Sauce

Makes 4 Servings.

8 ounces (225 g) semi-sweet chocolate, broken into pieces
1 cup (250 ml) heavy cream

1. Preheat the water bath to 140°F (60°C).
2. Put the chocolate and cream into a heat-stable, resealable pouch, squeeze out all the air, and seal.
3. Put the sealed pouch into the water bath and heat until the chocolate has melted, about 15 minutes.
4. Remove the pouch and massage or agitate until well mixed.
5. Serve immediately or hold it in the water bath until needed.

Caramel Sauce

Makes 4 Servings.

1 can (14 ounces/397 g) fat-free sweetened condensed milk
¼ teaspoon (1 ml) cider vinegar (optional)
1 pinch salt (optional)

1. Preheat the water bath to 175°(80°C).
2. Pour the condensed milk into a heat-stable, resealable pouch, squeeze out all the air, and seal.
3. Put the sealed pouch into the water bath and cook for 10–20 hours.
4. Remove the pouch from the water bath and pour into a bowl.
5. If desired, season with vinegar and salt.
6. Either serve immediately or store in the refrigerator until needed.

Fresh Yogurt

Makes 4–6 Servings

4 cups (1 l) milk

2 tablespoons (30 ml) active culture plain yogurt

1. Preheat the water bath to 113°F (45°C).

2. Scald and cool the milk before adding the yogurt to improve the texture of your yogurt.

    1. Microwave the milk in a microwave safe container until it reaches a light simmer at around 180–190°F (85–90°C).
    2. Cool the milk until it's no longer hot to the touch (at 115°F/45°C or less).

3. Mix the milk and yogurt in a quart (liter) canning jar and secure the lid tightly.

4. Set the canning jar into the preheated water bath, right side up, with a weight on top of the lid to keep it from falling over. The water level should be at or just above the height of the milk mixture in the jar. Let the mixture incubate until it sets, about 4–6 hours.

5. Transfer the yogurt to the refrigerator to firm up.

Appendix

Equipment

Sous vide cooking requires special equipment: a temperature controlled water bath; a vacuum sealing machine; and heat-stable, food-grade, plastic pouches.

The Water Bath

The essence of sous vide cooking is precise temperature control. While a determined cook can keep a large pot of water to within a few degrees (by checking the temperature every few minutes and adjusting the temperature with ice cubes and boiling water), it's incredibly tedious and error prone. The problem is that traditional heat sources aren't designed to cook food at its ideal temperature and frequently have temperature swings of 25–50°F (15–30°C). Thus, cooking food at its ideal temperature for hours or days necessitates the use of a sophisticated temperature controller that can keep the temperature of the water to within about 1°F (0.5°C). These sophisticated temperature controllers are typically proportional-integral-derivative (PID) controllers.

Sous vide cooking systems come in several guises: integrated one-piece units that house a water bath and an integrated PID-controlled heating element, such as the SousVide Supreme™; immersion circulators, in which the PID is integrated with the heating element and a small immersible pump circulates the water; or as a separate, external unit that controls another electronic device, such as a rice cooker or a slow cooker. For most home cooks, an integrated unit such as the SousVide Supreme is the best choice. It's less expensive than an immersion circulator and doesn't need to be manually tuned like an external PID controller—a process that can be quite time consuming.

Immersion circulators are the most versatile and expensive form of equipment used for sous vide cooking. They were designed for round-the-clock use in research laboratories that need to keep a liquid at a very precise and uniform temperature. Immersion circulators are composed of a self-tuning PID controller with a platinum resistance thermometer, a heating element that's immersed in the water, and a small pump that circulates the water to keep the temperature uniform throughout. The rugged construction and the ability to keep the water to within 0.1°F (0.05°C) of a set temperature has made immersion circulators the preferred choice in high-end restaurants. While any digital immersion circulator designed for the laboratory should work for sous vide cooking, the most popular brands used for culinary applications are PolyScience, Julabo, Techne, Lauda, Haake, and Roner. Such precision and ruggedness, however, are overkill in most home kitchens.

External PID-controllers measure the temperature of the water and use this information to decide how much power to give the appliance that they're controlling. So they can be used on only simple appliances with mechanical switches that won't be reset when the power is turned on-and-off. The most common appliances controlled by external PID-controllers are rice cookers, slow cookers, countertop food warmers (also known as steam tables), and roasters. Slow cookers and roasters have very poor water circulation and an aquarium air bubbler (or a small pump) must be used to agitate the water. Since the rate at which these various appliances heat and cool is different, the external PID-controller must be manually tuned[8] for each device. A word of caution: the tuning produced by the 'auto-tune' function on most controllers is poor and won't give the precision and reliability needed for optimal sous vide cooking. Also, the thermistor temperature sensors used in most external PID-controllers need to be recalibrated on a regular basis and can become erratic if placed in boiling water. After careful tuning and calibrating, an external PID-controller can usually keep the temperature of a water bath to within 1°F (0.5°C). The two most popular brands of external PID-controller for sous vide cooking are Fresh Meals Solutions and Auber Instruments.

Integrated water baths consist of a water bath with a built in heating element and a carefully tuned PID-controller. Unlike an external PID-controller, the manufacturer knows the heating and cooling characteristics of the water bath and is able to tune the PID-controller so that it's nearly as stable as an immersion circulator. In addition to the numerous integrated water baths designed for research laboratories, Eades Appliance Technology LLC designed the SousVide Supreme specifically for sous vide cooking; I feel that this unit is especially well designed and I recommend it highly.

Calibration

Calibration is extremely important because pasteurization times depend critically on temperature—a decrease in temperature of 2°F (1°C) increases the pasteurization time for poultry by about 50%![9] While it's unlikely that

---

[8] A simple way to manually tune your PID-controller is to: (1) set the I and D terms to zero; (2) check the temperature every five minutes for about an hour to see if the temperature oscillates; (3) if the temperature oscillates, double the value of P; (4) repeat steps (2) and (3); and, (5) when the temperature no longer oscillates, set the value of P to half its current value. Unless the temperature swings are more than 1°F (0.5°C), the I and D terms can remain set to zero.

[9] From the food safety chapter, we see that the z-value of *Listeria monocytogenes* in poultry is 5.66°C. Thus, the D-value at 59°C is 50% longer than at 60°C ($10^{1°C/5.66°C} = 1.50$).

you have a thermometer that's accurate to 0.2°F (0.1°C) in your kitchen, there is a good chance that you have one in your medicine cabinet.

To check the calibration of your water bath, set it to 100°F (37°C). Once the water bath has reached 100°F (37°C), wait 20–30 minutes and then measure the temperature of the water with an oral fever thermometer in several locations. If the temperature shown on the water bath's display is off by more than 1°F (0.5°C) from the temperature measured by your oral thermometer, you'll need to adjust the temperature that you set the water bath to appropriately. I recommend checking the calibration of your water bath at least once a month.

Plastic Pouches

Food cooked sous vide is vacuum-sealed in heat-stable, food-grade, plastic pouches. These plastic pouches must meet several specifications: they must be food-grade to limit the migration of plastic constituents into the food; they must be heat resistant with a softening point of 195°F (90°C) or higher; they should have a low gas permeability to prevent freezer burn on extended storage in a freezer; and they must have enough mechanical strength. There are various products available that meet these requirements in most grocery stores and online; if in doubt, please contact the manufacturer.

The pouches used in sous vide cooking fall into three categories: resealable pouches, clamp-style vacuum pouches and chamber-style vacuum pouches. High-end restaurants and commercial kitchens typically use inexpensive flat pouches that can be vacuum-sealed using only a very expensive chamber vacuum-sealer. Most home cooks use one of the following: a clamp-style vacuum-sealer, such as a FoodSaver® or SousVide Supreme Vacuum Sealer; a permeable membrane suction resealable pouch system, such as the FoodSaver MealSaver™ or Reynolds® Handi-Vac® or the Ziploc® vacuum system; or, resealable heavy-duty Ziploc freezer pouches. Clamp-style vacuum-sealers and permeable membrane suction sealers work best when there is little or no liquid in the pouch and resealable pouches work best when there is at least a quarter cup (60 ml) of liquid in the pouch.

Clamp-style vacuum-sealers use special pouches with a textured pattern that allows them to remove most the air from the pouch. Clamp-style vacuum-sealers work well, so long as there is little or no liquid in the pouch. If a recipe calls for more than a couple of tablespoons (20–30 ml) of liquid in the pouch, then you should either freeze the liquid, use a resealable pouch, or use a chamber vacuum-sealer. Please consult the user manual of your clamp-style vacuum-sealer for detailed instructions.

Resealable (heavy-duty freezer) pouches can be used if a recipe calls for a quarter cup (60 ml) or more liquid to be placed in the pouch. To remove most the air from the pouch, use the water displacement method as follows:

1. fill a deep container (such as a pan, pitcher, or bowl) with fresh cold water;

2. submerge the bottom of the unsealed pouch into the water until only the sealable top is above the surface of the water;

3. start sealing one side of the pouch and feeding the just sealed edge under the water as you go—when you have finished sealing the pouch, it should be completely submerged in the water; and

4. remove the pouch from the water and check that the seal is good and little or no air remains in the pouch.

When there is little or no liquid in the pouch, this water displacement method won't work and a clamp-style vacuum-sealer should be used instead.

Chamber vacuum-sealers work by removing the air from both the pouch and the chamber it's placed in. They're quite expensive because they use very powerful (and heavy) vacuum pumps and have to be designed to withstand around 14.7 pounds per square inch (1.0 bar) of pressure exerted by the atmosphere on the surface of the chamber. A chamber-style vacuum-sealer can do a few tricks that clamp-style vacuum-sealers and resealable pouches cannot. They can compress some fruits and vegetables. They can infuse some fruits, vegetables, and (to a lesser extent) meat with a flavored liquid (e.g., infuse fruit with alcohol, flash pickle cucumbers, and slightly improve marination). Additionally, they can de-gas liquids and purées to improve their texture and concentrate their flavors. While a chamber-style vacuum-sealer is a powerful tool in a high-end restaurant, it, too, is overkill in the typical home kitchen.

Food Safety

Most people learn about food safety from family members, the media, and (occasionally) from government publications. Unfortunately, most of this information is out-dated and some of it's potentially dangerous. This chapter briefly discusses food safety practices that are based on current scientific research..

Overview

Food safety is about minimizing risks—both real and perceived. While risk can never be completely eliminated, you can manage it by always following a few basic procedures:

- Buy fruits and vegetables that appear fresh.
- Buy meat, fish, and poultry that's within its 'sell-by' or 'use-by' date and that doesn't have a strong odor.
- Use the double hand wash technique before handling food.
- Wash your hands after handling unwashed or uncooked foods.
- Double wash fruits and vegetables just before eating—soak them in clean, cold water and then rinse them in a colander under running water.
- Wash and sanitize cutting boards and knives after cutting uncooked foods.
- Always cook meat, fish, and poultry to make them safe.
    Cook meat, fish, and poultry at or above 130°F (54.5°C) for long enough to reduce any infectious food pathogens (germs) to a safe level. See the tables in this chapter for recommended cooking times.
    Cut meat, fish, and poultry into small enough portions to ensure that the center of the food will reach 130°F (54.5°C) within 6 hours.
- Foods cooked sous vide can either be held at or above 130°F (54.5°C) until they're served or rapidly chilled in an ice water bath that's at least half ice, see Table 5 on page 259. Pouches that have been rapidly chilled food can either be:
    stored in a refrigerator for a few days or
    labeled and frozen indefinitely.

Controlling Food-Borne Risks

The hazards from consuming food come from several sources: food pathogens, chiefly bacteria; harmful chemicals; and hard foreign objects. Harmful chemicals include: natural toxins found in some plants or produced by some bacteria; chemical contaminants, such as pesticides and antibiotic residues; and food allergens, to which as many as 3½–4% of the population may be sensitive. Hard foreign objects include such things as bones, stones, pits, seeds, buckshot, and whole spices. Reducing the risk of food pathogens is achieved by selecting foods with low initial levels of contamination, reducing the level of contamination, and preventing the increase in the level of contamination.

Always buy food that appears fresh and is from a trusted source. Vegetables should never be limp. Fruits shouldn't be bruised or too ripe. Fish should still smell of the sea and have flesh that's shiny, moist, and firm to the touch. Meat should be within its 'sell-by' or 'use-by' date and shouldn't have a strong odor or feel slimy. Always refrigerate or freeze raw meat, fish, and poultry as soon as possible; in the refrigerator, store raw meat, fish, and poultry below fruits, vegetables, cooked foods, and ready-to-eat foods to prevent cross-contamination should they leak.

There are two types of hazards from food-borne pathogens: infection and intoxication. Food-borne infection occurs when food pathogens get past our bodies' formidable defenses and cause illness. Illness from food-borne infections typically take between a couple days and a week (such as for *Escherichia coli, Listeria monocytogenes, Campylobacter spp., Shigella spp., Yersinia enterocolitica,* and *Vibrio spp.*), but can take as little as 6 hours (such as for *Salmonella spp., Clostridium perfringens,* and *Bacillus cereus*) or as long as a couple of months (such as with Hepatitis A). Food-borne intoxication or poisoning occurs when toxins that are produced by some microorganisms as they multiply in the food are consumed. Symptoms from food-borne intoxication typically take 1–6 hours to occur (such as with *Clostridium botulinum, Bacillus cereus,* and *Staphylococcus aureus*). Food pathogens are distinct from both beneficial and spoilage microorganisms, so food pathogens and toxins cannot be seen, smelled, or tasted.

Although food pathogens could be controlled with the addition of acids, salts, and some spices, sous vide cooking relies on temperature control. Food pathogens can grow at temperatures between 29.3°F (−1.5°C) and 126.1°F (52.3°C). Heating food to reduce the level of vegetative food pathogens to a safe level is called pasteurization. Vegetative pathogens are simply active microorganisms that are growing and multiplying. Some bacterial food pathogens are also able to form spores that are very resistant to heat and chemicals. Heating food to reduce both the vegetative microorganisms and the spores to a safe level is called sterilization.[10]

Pasteurization is a combination of both temperature and time. Consider the common food pathogen *Salmonella spp.* At 140°F (60°C), all the *Salmonella* in a piece of ground beef doesn't die instantly—it is reduced

---

[10] Sterilization is typically achieved by using a pressure cooker to heat the center of the food to 250°F (121°C) for 2.4 minutes. Sterilized foods are shelf stable, but are grossly overcooked and taste similar to canned foods.

by a factor of ten every 2.76 minutes. It takes longer to destroy food pathogens at lower temperatures and less time at higher temperatures: it takes 15.2 minutes to reduce *Salmonella* by a factor ten at 130°F (54.5°C) and only 30 seconds at 150°F (65.5°C). The rate at which the pathogens die also depends on acidity, fat content, meat species, muscle type, salt content, certain spices, and water content. Pasteurized foods must either be eaten immediately or rapidly chilled and refrigerated to prevent the out-growth and multiplication of spores. Moreover, the center of the food should reach 130°F (54.5°C) within 6 hours to prevent the toxin producing pathogen *C. perfringens* from multiplying to dangerous levels. For specific pasteurization times, see Tables 2 to 4 starting on page 256.

Food Pathogens and Sous Vide Cooking

Sous vide processing is used in the food industry to extend the shelf-life of food products. When pasteurized sous vide pouches are held at below 38°F (3.3°C), they remain safe and palatable for three to four weeks. Unfortunately, less than 2% of household refrigerators spend all their time below 41°F (5°C). So, unless you have a very cold refrigerator, you can refrigerate foods cooked sous vide for only a few days.

Cook-Hold

The simplest and safest method of sous vide cooking is cook-hold—the raw (or partially cooked) ingredients are vacuum-sealed, pasteurized, and then held at 130°F (54.5°C) or above until served. While hot holding the food prevents food pathogens from growing, the food may become mushy if held for more than twice the recommended cooking times that start on page 22.

Cook-Chill and Cook-Freeze

The most popular methods of sous vide cooking in restaurants are cook-chill and cook-freeze: raw (or partially cooked) ingredients are vacuum-sealed, pasteurized, rapidly chilled (to avoid sporulation of *C. perfringens*), and either refrigerated or frozen until they're reheated at 130°F (54.5°C) or above for serving. The usual method for rapidly chilling food is to put the pouch(es) into an ice water bath that's at least half ice for the times listed in Table 5 on page 259.

For cook-chill sous vide, it's important that cooking achieves at least a six-decimal reduction in *Listeria monocytogenes*. *Listeria* is the most heat-resistant non-spore forming pathogen and is able to grow at refrigerator tempera-tures. Moreover, while keeping the food sealed in plastic pouches prevents recontamination after cooking, spores of *C. botulinum*, *C. perfringens*, and *B. cereus* can all survive the mild heat treatment of pasteurization. Therefore, after rapid chilling, the food must either be frozen or held at

- below 36.5°F (2.5°C) for up to 90 days,
- below 38°F (3.3°C) for less than 31 days,
- below 41°F (5°C) for less than 10 days, or
- below 44.5°F (7°C) for less than 5 days

to prevent spores of non-proteolytic *C. botulinum* from outgrowing and producing deadly neurotoxin. A few sous vide recipes use temperature-time combinations that can reduce non-proteolytic *C. botulinum* to a safe level; specifically, a 6D reduction in non-proteolytic *C. botulinum* requires 520 minutes (8 hours 40 minutes) at 167°F (75°C), 75 minutes at 176°F (80°C), or 25 minutes at 185°F (85°C). The food may then be stored at below 39°F (4°C) indefinitely, the minimum temperature at which *B. cereus* can grow.

Science: Computing Pasteurization Times

Recall that pasteurization depends on both temperature and time. At 140°F (60°C), *Listeria monocytogenes* is decreased by a factor of ten every 3.63 minutes. This is often referred to as a one decimal reduction and is written $D_{60}^{9.22} = 3.63$ minutes, where the subscript specifies the temperature (in °C) that the *D* value refers to and the superscript is the z-value (in °C). The z-value specifies how the D-value changes with temperature; increasing the temperature by the z-value decreases the time needed for a one decimal reduction by a factor ten. The classical model for the log reduction in pathogens is

$$LR = \frac{1}{D_{Ref}} \int_0^t 10^{(T(t') - T_{Ref})/z} \, dt'$$

where, for Listeria in meat, $D_{Ref} = 3.63$ minutes, $T_{Ref} = 40°F$ (60°C), $z = 16.6°F$ (9.22°C), and T is the core temperature of the meat.

The transfer of heat (by conduction) is described by the partial differential equation, $T_t = \nabla \cdot (\alpha \nabla T)$, where $\alpha \equiv k/(\rho C_p)$ is thermal diffusivity (m²/sec), k is thermal conductivity (W/m-K), ρ is density (kg/m³), and C_p is specific heat (kJ/kg-K). If we know the temperature at some initial time and can describe how the temperature at the surface changes, then we can uniquely determine T. Although k, ρ and C_p depend on position, time, and temperature, we will assume they're constant for thawed meat, fish, and poultry. Thermal diffusivity also depends on meat species, muscle type, and water content. Despite these variations in thermal diffusivity, we can always choose a (minimum) thermal diffusivity that will underestimate the temperature of the meat as it cooks (and overestimate the temperature as it cools). For the calculations in this cookbook, I assume the slowest heating shape (a slab) and use 1.11x10⁻⁷m²/sec for meat, 1.08x10⁻⁷m²/sec for poultry, and 0.995x 10⁻⁷m²/sec for fish, since most foods have thermal diffusivities between 1.2 and 1.6x10⁻⁷m²/sec.

Pasteurization Times for Fish in a 140°F (60°C) Water Bath

Thickness (inches)	Lean Time (minutes)	Fatty Time (minutes)	Thickness (inches)	Lean Time (hours)	Fatty Time (hours)
¼	20	30	1	1	1¼
½	30	40	1¼	1⅓	1⅔
¾	40	55	1½	1¾	2
			1¾	2¼	2½
			2	2¾	3
			2¼	3⅓	3¾
			2½	4	4½
(mm)	(minutes)	(minutes)	(mm)	(hours)	(hours)
5	15	30	25	1	1¼
10	25	35	30	1¼	1½
15	35	45	35	1½	1¾
20	45	55	40	2	2¼
			45	2⅓	2⅔
			50	2¾	3
			55	3¼	3½
			60	3⅔	4
			65	4¼	4⅔

Table 2. Pasteurization times for a 1,000,000:1 reduction of Listeria monocytogenes in finfish. Lean fish (such as cod) has D_{60} $5.59 = 2.88$ minutes, while fatty fish (such as salmon) has D_{60} $5.68 = 5.13$ minutes (Embarek and Huss, 1993). For additional pasteurization times-and-temperatures, see A Practical Guide to Sous Vide Cooking (Baldwin, 2008):
<http://www.douglasbaldwin.com/sous-vide.html>.

Pasteurization Times for Poultry in a 140°F (60°C) Water Bath

Thickness (inches)	Time (minutes)	Thickness (inches)	Time (hours)
¼	40	1	1⅓
½	50	1¼	1¾
¾	60	1½	2¼
		1¾	2⅔
		2	3¼
		2¼	3¾
		2½	4½
		2¾	5
(mm)	(minutes)	(mm)	(hours)
5	40	20	1
10	45	25	1⅓
15	50	30	1⅔
		35	2
		40	2⅓
		45	2⅔
		50	3
		55	3½
		60	4
		65	4⅔
		70	5¼

Table 3. Time required for a 1,000,000.1 reduction of Listeria monocytogenes in poultry. The times were computed using $D_{60}^{5.66} = 5.94$ minutes, which was calculated using linear regression from (O'Bryan et al., 2006, Table 2). For additional pasteurization times-and-temperatures, see A Practical Guide to Sous Vide Cooking (Baldwin, 2008):
<http://www.douglasbaldwin.com/sous-vide.html>.

Pasteurization Times for Meat

Water Bath:	130°F	140°F	Thickness	130°F	140°F
Thickness	Time	Time		Time	Time
(inches)	(hours)	(minutes)	(inches)	(hours)	(hours)
¼	1½	25	1½	2⅓	1¼
½	1½	30	1¾	2⅔	1½
¾	1⅔	35	2	3	1¾
1	1¾	45	2¼	3⅓	2
1¼	2	60	2½	3¾	2⅓
			2¾	4	2¾
Water Bath:	55°C	60°C	Thickness	55°C	60°C
Thickness	Time	Time		Time	Time
(mm)	(hours)	(minutes)	(mm)	(hours)	(hours)
5	1¼	25	35	2	1
10	1⅓	25	40	2¼	1¼
15	1½	30	45	2½	1½
20	1½	40	50	2¾	1¾
25	1⅔	45	55	3	2
30	1¾	55	60	3⅓	2¼
			65	3½	2½
			70	4	2¾

Table 4. Times required to reduce Listeria monocytogenes in thawed meat by 1,000,000:1. These times are computed using $D_{60}9.22 = 3.63$ minutes, which was calculated using linear regression from (O'Bryan et al., 2006, Table 1), (Bolton et al., 2000, Table 2), and (Hansen and Knøchel, 1996, Table 1). For additional pasteurization times-and-temperatures, see A Practical Guide to Sous Vide Cooking (Baldwin, 2008):
<http://www.douglasbaldwin.com/sous-vide.html>.

Cooling Times in Ice Water

Thickness (inches)	Time (minutes)	Thickness (inches)	Time (hours)
¼	2	1½	1¼
½	10	1¾	1⅔
¾	20	2	2
1	30	2¼	2⅔
1¼	50	2½	3⅓
		2¾	4
(mm)	**(minutes)**	**(mm)**	**(hours)**
5	1	35	1
10	5	40	1⅓
15	10	45	1⅔
20	20	50	2
25	30	55	2½
30	45	60	3
		65	3½
		70	4

Table 5. Approximate cooling times for the core temperature of the food to reach 41°F (5°C) in an ice water bath that is at least half ice.

Select Bibliography

For General Readers

Harold McGee. *On Food and Cooking: The Science and Lore of The Kitchen.* Scribner, New York, 2004.

Hervé This. *Molecular Gastronomy: Exploring the Science of Flavor.* Columbia University Press, New York, 2006.

Cookbooks and Websites with Sous Vide Recipes

Grant Achatz. *Alinea.* Ten Speed Press, 2008.

Douglas E. Baldwin. *A Practical Guide to Sous Vide Cooking.* 2008, <http://www.douglasbaldwin.com/sous-vide.html>.

Heston Blumenthal. *The Big Fat Duck Cookbook.* Bloomsbury, 2008.

Thomas Keller, Jonathan Benno, Corey Lee, and Sebastien Rouxel. *Under Pressure: Cooking Sous Vide.* Artisan, 2008.

Nils Norén and Dave Arnold. *Cooking Issues: The French Culinary Institute's Tech'N Stuff Blog.* 2009, <http://cookingissues.wordpress.com/>.

Joan Roca and Salvador Brugués. *Sous-Vide Cuisine.* Montagud Editores, S.A., 2005.

Sous Vide: Recipes, Techniques & Equipment. eGullet Society for Culinary Arts & Letters' Forum. 2004, <http://forums.egullet.org/index.php?/topic/116617-sous-vide-recipes-techniques-equipment/>.

Food Safety

O. Peter Snyder, Jr. *Food safety hazards and controls for the home food preparer.* Technical report, Hospitality Institute of Technology and Management, 2006, <http://www.hi-tm.com/homeprep/Home-2006-2col-forpdf.pdf>.

For Specialized and Technical Readers

Peter Barham, Leif H. Skibsted, Wender L. P. Bredie, Michael Bom Frøst, Per Møller, Jens Risbo, Pia Snitkjær, and Louise Mørch Mortensen. Molecular gastronomy: a new emerging scientific discipline. *Chemical Reviews,* doi: 10.1021/cr900105w, 2010.

H.-D. Belitz, W. Grosch, and P. Schieberle. *Food Chemistry.* Springer, 3rd edition, 2004.

Helen Charley. *Food Science.* John Wiley and Sons, second edition, 1982.

R. A. Lawrie. *Lawrie's Meat Science.* CRC, 6th edition, 1998.

Taste, Texture, and Nutrition

Gillian A. Armstrong and Heather McIlveen. Effects of prolonged storage on the sensory quality and consumer acceptance of sous vide meat-based recipe dishes. *Food Quality and Preference,* 11:377–385, 2000.

J. A. Beltran, M. Bonnet, and A. Ouali. Collagenase effect on thermal denaturation of intramuscular collagen. *Journal of Food Science,* 56(6): 1497–1499, 1991.

P. E. Bouton and P. V. Harris. Changes in the tenderness of meat cooked at 50–65°C. *Journal of Food Science*, 46:475–478, 1981.

Ivor Church. The sensory quality, microbiological safety and shelf life of packaged foods. In Sue Ghazala, editor, *Sous Vide and Cook–Chill Processing for the Food Industry*, pages 190–205. Aspen Publishers, Gaithersburg, Maryland, 1998.

Ivor J. Church and Anthony L. Parsons. The sensory quality of chicken and potato products prepared using cook-chill and sous vide methods. *International Journal of Food Science and Technology*, 35:155–162, 2000.

Philip G. Creed. The sensory and nutritional quality of 'sous vide' foods. *Food Control*, 6(1):45–52, 1995.

Philip G. Creed. Sensory and nutritional aspects of sous vide processed foods. In Sue Ghazala, editor, *Sous Vide and Cook–Chill Processing for the Food Industry*, pages 57–88. Aspen Publishers, Gaithersburg, Maryland, 1998.

C. Lester Davey, Alan F. Niederer, and Arie E. Graafhuis. Effects of ageing and cooking on the tenderness of beef muscle. *Journal of the Science of Food and Agriculture*, 27:251–256, 1976.

J. D. Fagan and T. R. Gormley. Effect of sous vide cooking, with freezing, on selected quality parameters of seven fish species in a range of sauces. *European Food Research and Technology*, 220:299–304, 2005.

M. C. García-Linares, E. Gonzalez-Fandos, M. C. García-Fernández, and M. T. García-Arias. Microbiological and nutritional quality of sous vide or traditionally processed fish: Influence of fat content. *Journal of Food Quality*, 27:371–387, 2004.

P. García-Segovia, A. Andrés-Bello, and J. Martínez-Monzó. Effect of cooking method on mechanical properties, color and structure of beef muscle (*M. pectoralis*). *Journal of Food Engineering*, 80.813–821, 2007.

S. Ghazala, J. Aucoin, and T. Alkanani. Pasteurization effect on fatty acid stability in a sous vide product containing seal meat (*Phoca groenlandica*). *Journal of Food Science*, 61(3):520–523, 1996.

E. González-Fandos, M. C. García-Linares, A. Villarino-Rodríguez, M. T. García-Arias, and M. C. García-Fernández. Evaluation of the microbiological safety and sensory quality of rainbow trout (*Oncorhynchus mykiss*) processed by the sous vide method. *Food Microbiology*, 21:193–201, 2004.

E. González-Fandos, A. Villarino-Rodríguez, M. C. García-Linares, M. T. García-Arias, and M. C. García-Fernández. Microbiological safety and sensory characteristics of salmon slices processed by the sous vide method. *Food Control*, 16:77–85, 2005.

N. Graiver, A. Pinotti, A. Califano, and N. Zaritzky. Diffusion of sodium chloride in pork tissue. *Journal of Food Engineering*, 77:910–918, 2006.

Tina B. Hansen, Susanne Knøchel, Dorte Juncher, and Grete Bertelsen. Storage characteristics of sous vide cooked roast beef. *International Journal of Food Science and Technology*, 30:365–378, 1995.

Select Bibliography

Anne Lassen, Morten Kall, Kirsten Hansen, and Lars Ovesen. A comparison of the retention of vitamins B1, B2 and B6, and cooking yield in pork loin with conventional and enhanced meal-service systems. *European Food Research and Technology*, 215:194–199, 2002.

Lene Meinert, Annette Schäfer, Charlotte Bjergegaard, Margit D. Aaslyng, and Wender L. P. Bredie. Comparison of glucose, glucose 6-phosphate, ribose, and mannose as flavour precursors in pork; the effect of monosaccharide addition on flavour generation. *Meat Science*, 81:419–425, 2009.

Anne Meynier and Donald S. Mottram. The effect of pH on the formation of volatile compounds in meat-related model systems. *Food Chemistry*, 52: 361–366, 1995.

Donald S. Mottram. Flavour formation in meat and meat products: A review. *Food Chemistry*, 62(4):415–424, 1998.

Donald S. Mottram and Frank B. Whitfield. Volatile compounds from the reaction of cysteine, ribose, and phospholipid in low-moisture systems. *Journal of Agriculture and Food Chemistry*, 43(4):984–988, 1995.

A. D. Neklyudov. Nutritive fibers of animal origin: Collagen and its fractions as essential components of new and useful food products. *Applied Biochemistry and Microbiology*, 39:229–238, 2003.

T. H. Powell, M. E. Dikeman, and M. C. Hunt. Tenderness and collagen composition of beef semi-tendinosus roasts cooked by conventional convective cooking and modeled, multi-stage, convective cooking. *Meat Science*, 55:421–425, 2000.

Mia Schellekens. New research issues in sous-vide cooking. *Trends in Food Science and Technology*, 7:256–262, 1996.

M. V. Simpson, J. P. Smith, B. K. Simpson, H. Ramaswamy, and K. L. Dodds. Storage studies on a sous vide spaghetti and meat sauce product. *Food Microbiology*, 11:5–14, 1994.

Tonje Holte Stea, Madelene Johansson, Margaretha Jägerstad, and Wenche Frølich. Retention of folates in cooked, stored and reheated peas, broccoli and potatoes for use in modern large-scale service systems. *Food Chemistry*, 101:1095–1107, 2006.

E. Tornberg. Effect of heat on meat proteins—implications on structure and quality of meat products. *Meat Science*, 70:493–508, 2005.

Sergio R. Vaudagna, Guillermo Sánchez, Maria S. Neira, Ester M. Insani, Alyandra B. Picallo, Maria M. Gallinger, and Jorge A. Lasta. Sous vide cooked beef muscles: Effects of low temperature-long time (LT-LT) treatments on their quality characteristics and storage stability. *International Journal of Food Science and Technology*, 37:425–441, 2002.

J. F. Vélez-Ruiz, F. T. Vergara-Balderas, M. E. Sosa-Morales, and J. Xique-Hernández. Effect of temperature on the physical properties of chicken strips during deep-fat frying. *International Journal of Food Properties*, 5(1):127–144, 2002.

Food Safety

Annika Andersson, Ulf Rönner, and Per Einar Granum. What problems does the food industry have with the spore-forming pathogens Bacillus cereus and Clostridium perfringens? International Journal of Food Microbiology, 28:145–155, 1995.

Necla Aran. The effect of calcium and sodium lactates on growth from spores of Bacillus cereus and Clostridium perfringens in a 'sous-vide' beef goulash under temperature abuse. International Journal of Food Microbiology, 63:117–123, 2001.

P. Arvidsson, M. A. J. S. Van Boekel, K. Skog, and M. Jägerstad. Kineteics of formation of polar heterocyclic amines in a meat model system. Journal of Food Science, 62(5):911–916, 1997.

R. Graham Bell, Nicholass Penney, and Sandra M. Moorhead. Growth of the psychrotrophic pathogens Aeromonas hydrophila, Listeria monocytogenes and Yersinia enterocolitica on smoked blue cod (Parapercis colias) packed under vacuum or carbon dioxide. International Journal of Food Science and Technology, 30(4):515–521, 1995.

G. D. Betts and J. E. Gaze. Growth and heat resistance of psychrotropic Clostridium botulinum in relation to 'sous vide' products. Food Control, 6.57–63, 1995.

Arun K. Bhunia. Foodborne Microbial Pathogens. Food Science Text Series. Springer, 2008.

D. J. Bolton, C. M. McMahon, A. M. Doherty, J. J. Sheridan, D. A. McDowell, I. S. Blair, and D. Harrington. Thermal inactivation of Listeria monocytogenes and Yersinia enterocolitica in minced beef under laboratory conditions and in sous-vide prepared minced and solid beef cooked in a commercial retort. Journal of Applied Microbiology, 88: 626 632, 2000.

Peter Karim Ben Embarek and Hans Henrik Huss. Heat resistance of Listeria monocytogenes in vacuum packaged pasteurized fish fillets. International Journal of Food Microbiology, 20:85–95, 1993.

Judith Evans. Consumer perceptions and practice in the handling of chilled foods. In Sue Ghazala, editor, Sous Vide and Cook–Chill Processing for the Food Industry, pages 1–24. Aspen Publishers, Gaithersburg, Maryland, 1998.

Pablo S. Fernández and Michael W. Peck. A predictive model that describes the effect of prolonged heating at 70 to 90°C and subsequent incubation at refrigeration temperatures on growth from spores and toxigenesis by nonpro teolytic Clostridium botulinum in the presence of lysozyme. Applied and Environmental Microbiology, 65(8):3449–3457, 1999.

A. H. Geeraerd, C. H. Herremans, and J. F. Van Impe. Structural model requirements to describe microbial inactivation during a mild heat treatment. International Journal of Food Microbiology, 59:185–209, 2000.

G. W. Gould. Sous vide food: Conclusions of an ECFF Botulinum working party. Food Control, 10:47–51, 1999.

Select Bibliography

T. B. Hansen and S. Knøchel. Thermal inactivation of *Listeria monocytogenes* during rapid and slow heating in sous vide cooked beef. *Letters in Applied Microbiology*, 22:425–428, 1996.

J. Andrew Hudson, Sandra J. Mott, and Nicholass Penney. Growth of *Listeria monocytogenes*, *Aeromonas hydrophila*, and *Yersinia enterocolitica* on vacuum and saturated carbon dioxide controlled atmosphere-packaged sliced roast beef. *Journal of Food Protection*, 57(3):204–208, 1994.

M. Jägerstad, K. Skog, P. Arvidsson, and A. Solyakov. Chemistry, formation and occurrence of genotoxic heterocyclic amines identified in model systems and cooked foods. *Z Lebensm Unters Forsch A*, 207:419–427, 1998.

M. A. E. Johansson, L. Fredholm, I. Bjerne, and M. Jägerstad. Influence of frying fat on the formation of heterocyclic amines in fried beefburgers and pan residues. *Food and Chemical Toxicology*, 33(12): 993–1004, 1995.

V. K. Juneja, B. S. Eblen, and G. M. Ransom. Thermal inactivation of *Salmonella spp.* in chicken broth, beef, pork, turkey, and chicken: Determination of D- and z-values. *Journal of Food Science*, 66:146–152, 2001a.

V. K. Juneja, J. S. Novak, B. S. Eblen, and B. A. McClane. Heat resistance of *Clostridium perfringens* vegetative cells as affected by prior heat shock. *Journal of Food Safety*, 21(2):127–139, 2001b.

Vijay K. Juneja and John N. Sofos. *Control of Foodborne Microorganisms*, volume 114 of *Food Science and Technology*. Marcel Dekker, Inc., New York, 2002.

V. K. Juneja, R. C. Whiting, H. M. Marks, and O. P. Snyder. Predictive model for growth of *Clostridium perfringens* at temperatures applicable to cooling of cooked meat. *Food Microbiology*, 16(4):335–349, 1999.

Norman G. Marriott and Robert B. Gravani. *Principles of Food Sanitation*. Springer, 5th edition, 2006.

Ban Mishu, J. Koehler, L.A. Lee, D. Rodrigue, F.H. Brenner, P. Blake, and R. V. Tauxe. Outbreaks of *Salmonella enteritidis* infections in the United States, 1985-1991. *Journal of Infectious Diseases*, 169:547–552, 1994.

D. A. A. Mossel and Corry B. Struijk. Public health implication of refrigerated pasteurized ('sous-vide') foods. *International Journal of Food Microbiology*, 13:187–206, 1991.

R. Y. Murphy, L. K. Duncan, B. L. Beard, and K. H. Driscoll. D and z values of *Salmonella, Listeria innocua*, and *Listeria monocytogenes* in fully cooked poultry products. *Journal of Food Science*, 68(4):1443–1447, 2003.

National Advisory Committee on Microbiological Criteria for Food. Response to the questions posed by the food and drug administration and the national marine fisheries service regarding determination of cooking parameters for safe seafood for consumers. *Journal of Food Protection*, 71(6):1287–1308, 2008.

Hilda Nyati. An evaluation of the effect of storage and processing temperatures on the microbiological status of sous vide extended shelf-life products.

Food Control, 11:471–476, 2000a.

Hilda Nyati. Survival characteristics and the applicability of predictive mathematical modelling to *Listeria monocytogenes* growth in sous vide products. *International Journal of Food Microbiology*, 56: 123–132, 2000b.

Corliss A. O'Bryan, Philip G. Crandall, Elizabeth M. Martin, Carl L. Griffis, and Michael G. Johnson. Heat resistance of *Salmonella spp.*, *Listeria monocytogenes, Escherichia coli O157:H7*, and *Listeria innocua M1*, a potential surrogate for Listeria monocytogenes, in meat and poultry: A review. *Journal of Food Science*, 71(3):R23–R30, 2006.

Fiach C. O'Mahony, Tomás C. O'Riordan, Natalia Papkovskaia, Vladimir I. Ogurtsov, Joe P. Kerry, and Dmitri B. Papkovsky. Assessment of oxygen levels in convenience-style muscle-based sous vide products through optical means and impact on shelf-life stability. *Packaging Technology and Science*, 17:225–234, 2004.

Michael W. Peck. *Clostridium botulinum* and the safety of refrigerated processed foods of extended durability. *Trends in Food Science Technology*, 8:186–192, 1997.

Michael W. Peck and Sandra C. Stringer. The safety of pasteurised in-pack chilled meat products with respect to the foodborne botulism hazard. *Meat Science*, 70:461–475, 2005.

Svetlana Rybka-Rodgers. Improvement of food safety design of cook-chill foods. *Food Research International*, 34:449–455, 2001.

Svetlana Rybka-Rodgers. Developing a HACCP plan for extended shelf life cook-chill ready-to-eat meals. *Food Australia*, 51:430–433, 1999.

J. D. Schuman, B. W. Sheldon, J. M. Vandepopuliere, and H. R. Ball, Jr. Immersion heat treatments for inactivation of Salmonella enteritidis with intact eggs. *Journal of Applied Microbiology*, 83:438–444, 1997.

S. P. Shoemaker and M. D. Pierson. "Phoenix phenomenon" in the growth of *Clostridium perfringens*. *Applied and Environmental Microbiology*, 32(6): 803–807, 1976.

K. Skog. Cooking procedures and food mutagens: A literature review. *Food and Chemical Toxicology*, 31(9):655–675, 1993.

K. Skog, M. Jägerstad, and A. Laser Reutersward. Inhibitory effect of carbohydrates on the formation of mutagens in fried beef patties. *Food and Chemical Toxicology*, 30(8).681–688, 1992.

United States. Food Safety and Inspection Service. *Time-temperature tables for cooking ready-to-eat poultry products*. Notice 16-05, 2005.

United States. Department of Health and Human Services. Public Health Service. Food and Drug Administration. *Food code*. 2009.

R. R. Willardsen, F. F. Busta, C. E. Allen, and L. B. Smith. Growth and survival of *Clostridium perfringens* during constantly rising temperatures. Journal of Food Science, 43:470–475, 1977.

Select Bibliography

Heat Transfer in Food

J. De Baerdemaeker and B. M. Nicolaï. Equipment considerations for sous vide cooking. *Food Control*, 6(4):229–236, 1995.

Karl Mc Donald, Da-Wen Sun, and James G. Lyng. Effect of vacuum cooling on the thermophysical properties of a cooked beef product. *Journal of Food Engineering*, 52:167–176, 2002.

Lihan Huang. Computer simulation of heat transfer during in-package pasteurization of beef frankfurters by hot water immersion. *Journal of Food Engineering*, 80:839–849, 2007.

M. Kent, K. Christiansen, I. A. van Haneghem, E. Holtz, M. J. Morley, P. Nesvadba, and K. P. Poulsen. COST 90 collaborative measurement of thermal properties of foods. *Journal of Food Engineering*, 3:117–150, 1984.

Marek Markowski, Ireneusz Bialobrzewski, Marek Cierach, and Agnieszka Paulo. Determination of thermal diffusivity of lyoner type sausages during water bath cooking and cooling. *Journal of Food Engineering*, 65: 591–598, 2004.

Harold McGee, Jack McInerney and Alain Harrus. The virtual cook: Modeling heat transfer in the kitchen. *Physics Today*, 52:30–36, 1999.

B. M. Nicolaï and J. De Baerdemaeker. Sensitivity analysis with respect to the surface heat transfer coefficient as applied to thermal process calculations. *Journal of Food Engineering*, 28:21–33, 1996.

P. D. Sanz, M. D. Alonso, and R. H. Mascheroni. Thermophysical properties of meat products: General bibliography and experimental values. *Transactions of the ASAE*, 30:283–289 & 296, 1987.

M. A. Sheard and C. Rodger. Optimum heat treatments for 'sous vide' cook-chill products. *Food Control*, 6:53–56, 1995.

P. S. Sheridan and N. C. Shilton. Determination of the thermal diffusivity of ground beef patties under infrared radiation oven-shelf cooking. *Journal of Food Engineering*, 52:39–45, 2002.

R. P. Singh. Thermal diffusivity in food processing. Food Technology, 36 (2):134–137, 1982.

Kritsna Siripon, Ampawan Tansakul, and Gauri S. Mittal. Heat transfer modeling of chicken cooking in hot water. *Food Research International*, 40:923–930, 2007.

María Elena Sosa-Morales, Ronald Orzuna-Espíritu, and Jorge F. Vélez-Ruiz. Mass, thermal and quality aspects of deep-fat frying of pork meat. *Journal of Food Engineering*, 77:731–738, 2006.

Shwu-Jene Tsai, Nan Unklesbay, Kenneth Unklesbay, and Andrew Clarke. Thermal properties of restructured beef products at different isothermal temperatures. *Journal of Food Science*, 63(3):481–484, 1998.

Index

Index

Cover and book design by Faith Keating.

ISBN: 978-0-9844936-0-9

Printed in China.

Second edition, 2013.

1 2 3 4 5 6 7 8 9 10

Paradox Press

774 Mays Blvd, Suite 10-268
Incline Village NV 89451